PROTECTING CHILDREN AND YOUNG PEOPLE
Child Protection, Public Health and Nursing

PROTECTING CHILDREN AND YOUNG PEOPLE
SERIES EDITORS
JOHN DEVANEY
School of Sociology, Social Policy and Social Work, Queen's
University Belfast
and JULIE TAYLOR
School of Health and Population Sciences, University of Birmingham
and SHARON VINCENT
Social Work and Communities, Northumbria University

Child Protection, Public Health and Nursing

Edited by

Jane V. Appleton

Faculty of Health and Life Sciences,
Oxford Brookes University

and Sue Peckover

Faculty of Health and Wellbeing,
Sheffield Hallam University

DUNEDIN

EDINBURGH ◆ LONDON

Published by Dunedin Academic Press Limited

Head Office:
Hudson House, 8 Albany Street, Edinburgh EH1 3QB

London Office:
352 Cromwell Tower, Barbican, London EC2Y 8NB

bitlit

A **free** eBook edition is available
with the purchase of this print book.

CLEARLY PRINT YOUR NAME ABOVE IN UPPER CASE
Instructions to claim your free eBook edition:
1. Download the BitLit app for Android or iOS
2. Write your name in **UPPER CASE** on the line
3. Use the BitLit app to submit a photo
4. Download your eBook to any device

ISBNs:
978–1–78046–045–1 (Paperback)
978–1–78046–547–0 (ePub)
978–1–78046–548–7 (Kindle edition)
ISSN: 1756–0691

© Dunedin Academic Press 2015

The right of Jane V Appleton, Sue Peckover and the contributors to be identified as the authors of their parts of this work has been asserted by them in accordance with sections 77 and 78 of the Copyright, Designs and Patents Act 1988

British Library Cataloguing in Publication data
A catalogue record for this book is available from the British Library

Typeset by Makar Publishing Production, Edinburgh, Scotland
Printed in Great Britain by CPI Antony Rowe

Mixed Sources
Product group from well-managed
forests and other controlled sources
www.fsc.org Cert no. TT-COC-2082
© 1996 Forest Stewardship Council
FSC

CONTENTS

ACKNOWLEDGEMENTS

Thank you to Sarah Howcutt who helped with formatting our first draft.

THE CONTRIBUTORS

Jane V. Appleton is Professor of Primary and Community Care at Oxford Brookes University. Jane's research interests focus on health visiting, safeguarding children and child protection systems.

Dr Caroline Bradbury-Jones is Reader in Nursing at the University of Birmingham. She has a clinical background in health visiting. Her primary areas of research interest are in relation to vulnerable families and domestic violence and abuse.

Dr Eija Paavilainen is Professor of Nursing Science at the School of Health Sciences, University of Tampere, Finland. Her research interests focus upon family violence, child maltreatment and family risks.

Dr Sue Peckover is Senior Lecturer in Health Visiting at Sheffield Hallam University. Her research interests include public health, safeguarding children, domestic abuse, e-technologies and inter-professional knowledge and practices.

Dr Catherine Powell is a freelance Safeguarding Children Consultant and a Visiting Academic at the University of Southampton. Her career has embraced clinical practice, leadership, academia and national policy.

Dr Suzanne Smith has specialised in safeguarding in the NHS (National Health Service) for twenty years. A registered nurse and health visitor, Suzanne is currently Assistant Director of Nursing (Safeguarding) at a large acute trust.

Julie Taylor is Professor of Child Protection at the University of Birmingham. She is a nurse scientist whose research programme focuses on the wellbeing of vulnerable children and their families.

GLOSSARY OF ABBREVIATIONS

ACE	Adverse Childhood Experiences
CAADA	Coordinated Action against Domestic Abuse
CCG	Clinical Commissioning Groups
CCN	Children's Community Nurse
CPC	Child protection conference
CPHVA	Community Practitioners' and Health Visitors' Association
DH	Department of Health
ECI	European Competence Initiative
EU	European Union
FGM	Female genital mutilation
HCP	Healthy Child Programme
ISPCAN	International Society for the Prevention of Child Abuse & Neglect
LSCB	Local Safeguarding Children Board
NHS	National Health Service
NICE	National Institute for Health and Clinical Excellence
NMC	Nursing and Midwifery Council
NSPCC	National Society for the Prevention of Cruelty to Children
PHE	Public Health England
RCM	Royal College of Midwives
RCN	Royal College of Nursing
RCPCH	Royal College of Paediatrics and Child Health
SBAR	Situation, Background, Assessment, Recommendation
SCPHN	Specialist Community Public Health Nurses
SCR	Serious case review
SWOT	Strengths, weaknesses, opportunities and threats
WHO	World Health Organization

FOREWORD

Following the 2015 general election, with a new government in post, the revision of the *Working Together* guidance and the recent revelations of historic abuse leading to major enquiries and consideration of current practice, *Child Protection, Public Health and Nursing* is a welcome and timely publication. The authors and their fellow contributors remind us that nursing staff have a critical role in safeguarding and protecting children and also in contributing to a public health agenda that should embrace tackling child abuse and neglect. This book, aimed at nurses, health visitors and those working in child protection, helpfully discusses what is meant by the public health framework and why our strategy for preventing child maltreatment has to be framed in this way. *Child Protection, Public Health and Nursing* also looks at the challenges and difficulties that nurses face in safeguarding children and suggests possible solutions. As public health nurses, there is no doubt that health visitors particularly have a critical role to play.

I have long been a supporter of the work of health visitors, school nurses, community nurses and a range of other nurses in meeting the needs of families, protecting children and preventing abuse. The universal nature of nursing provision – or variations of that universalism, as described in this book – mean that the service reaches all children and young people and their families and is delivered in non-stigmatising ways. The culture of some professional groups creates barriers between themselves and their service users in contrast to nurses who can be more accessible. Nurses spend greater amounts of time with families, children and young people, affording opportunities for health visitors and nurses to build relationships, and both observe their families and the conditions in which they are living and identify causes for concern.

A number of years ago, with my colleague Jane Naish, I co-edited a series of papers which were published in *Key Issues in Child Protection for Health Visitors and Nurses* (Naish and Cloke, 1992). At the time we were generally optimistic that health visitors, school nurses and other nurses could positively progress safeguarding. We noted that the Children Act 1989, recently passed, had the potential to shift professional attitudes and organisational cultures. Preventive services were seen as important. The focus on children's rights and the paramountcy principle should have led to a greater focus on the child. There was a greater emphasis than ever before on professionals working together and on inter-agency collaboration. The principles and building blocks were sound.

Over the past twenty-five years there have been some improvements in safeguarding nursing practice, and *Child Protection, Public Health and Nursing* provides a number of good examples from across the family of nursing. The general direction has been positive. However this is not to deny that on occasions there have been shortcomings and that practice has fallen short of the ideal. Serious case reviews (SCRs) point to these failings. Child protection is complex, and nurses like all professionals face difficult decisions and dilemmas. They do not and should not operate in a vacuum. The authors and their contributors to *Child Protection, Public Health and Nursing* discuss these complexities.

Health visiting has not always been able to deliver on the preventive agenda and some of the reasons for this are clear. Appleton points out that for over some twenty years there was significant disinvestment in health visiting. This had a major impact on the profession, and while the policy has now been reversed, as is evident in the 2011 *Health Visitor Implementation Plan: A Call to Action* (DH, 2011), it is taking time for health visiting to recover.

Recent years have seen child poverty biting into the hearts of many communities, and this has placed huge pressures on families. Poverty, poor housing conditions and unemployment contribute to family stress and ill health, and the maltreatment of children can be a consequence. In turn, pressure is placed on health visiting, and community nursing caseloads and the family relationships and dynamics acquire additional complexities which pose challenges to professionals.

In these circumstances there is a risk that preventive strategies and activities are squeezed out. The National Society for the Prevention of

Cruelty to Children (NSPCC) is committed to the promotion of early intervention and believes that this is critical in ensuring that children and young people are protected and abuse prevented. And yet our *How Safe Are Our Children?* (Jütte *et al.*, 2014) research indicates that, while the past five years have seen many reports recommending early intervention and government and agencies endorsing the approach, the reality does not match the rhetoric. During this period the resources available for early intervention have arguably decreased rather than increased.

The challenges facing health visitors, community and other nurses continue to be great. They have a significant role to play in progressing the public health agenda, delivering early intervention and ensuring the effective protection of children and young people. Of course meeting the needs of families and children does not and should not fall to the nursing professions alone, and working together across professions and agencies is an imperative, as this book emphasises. Each individual profession needs to ensure that their practice is delivered to a high standard, and I believe that *Child Protection, Public Health and Nursing* will help inspire nurses to achieve this. Appleton and Peckover show that nurses have a great deal about which to be proud and that 'often small acts involving anticipatory guidance, prevention or early detection can make a big difference – and nurses can do this well'.

For our part, we at the NSPCC endorse the public health approach to tackling child abuse and neglect, and we call for greater early intervention. A number of our services, particularly our programme for supporting children under one and their families, are taking a preventive approach and working with nurses and health visitors. We have a common agenda and a commitment to sharing the learning from our services. We would welcome the opportunity to support nurses in their endeavours to prevent abuse and protect children. Together we can ensure that every childhood is worth fighting for.

Christopher Cloke
Head of Child Protection Awareness, NSPCC
Vice President, Community Practitioners' and Health Visitors' Association

CHAPTER 1

Child protection, public health and nursing

Jane V. Appleton, Oxford Brookes University
Sue Peckover, Sheffield Hallam University

Introduction

This chapter will provide an overview of the key role and contribution that nurses have in protecting children and young people, across the UK and in broader contexts. It will define child protection, safeguarding and public health, and briefly outline the legislative and policy context in which nurses work, before moving on to provide an overview of each of the chapters in the rest of this book.

All children and young people have a right to be protected from exploitation, child abuse and neglect. The UK, like many other Western countries, has invested heavily over the last fifteen years in a range of policy and multi-agency practice initiatives geared to address issues of child maltreatment and to promote child well-being. Yet child maltreatment continues to be a very significant public health and societal issue and a major concern globally. Cases of maltreatment of children and young people continue to hit the headlines, alongside official failures at all levels. Recent cases such as the deaths of Daniel Pelka, Hamzah Khan and Keanu Williams, institutional abuse within the Catholic church, the Savile Investigation and a series of high-profile trials across the UK concerned with child sexual exploitation all highlight the extent to which child maltreatment permeates our society.

Nurses, midwives and health visitors as frontline healthcare professionals have a key role to play in the protection of children and young people. Whatever settings nurses are working in, whether it be in acute hospital settings or in public health roles in primary care, nurses may have contact with children and their parents or carers. Thus all nurses have a potential role in identifying infants, children and young people at risk of abuse and neglect. In the UK the Nursing and Midwifery Council (NMC) professional code and standards of professional conduct highlight the nurse's duty of 'care and safety' to those in his/her care (NMC, 2015). Implicit within this is a requirement for nurses to know when a child or young person may be in need of early help and how to act on concerns that a child or young person may be suffering, or likely to suffer, significant harm through abuse and/or neglect (HM Government,

2015). In addition, policy is increasingly emphasising the importance of primary prevention of child maltreatment, and, for public health nurses in particular, opportunities to promote prevention start early: for example, in schools during health promotion activities and working with parents around the transition to parenthood. This book brings together a series of chapters which explore the important contribution of the nursing workforce to the prevention of child abuse and neglect, and the protection of children. The focus is largely on England, but also draws upon examples from the wider UK and European contexts.

Key Concepts
Child maltreatment

This concept has broadened in scope as knowledge has expanded/ increased about the wide range of abuse and neglect facing children and young people. Child maltreatment is a major public health and social-welfare imperative and a global problem. The considerable international interest in this area reflects the fact that child maltreatment occurs in all cultures and countries across the globe and across all social groups (WHO, 2006). It is a common problem which can result in death or serious injury and can also have severe long-term consequences that affect the child's life into adulthood, their family and society (Gilbert *et al.*, 2009a). Child maltreatment is also an extremely complex issue, which is not easy to define or measure (Corby *et al.*, 2012). It is a complex social construct, often with multi-factorial causes, and is regarded as 'a highly contentious and contested area' (Parton *et al.*, 1997, p. 70; Parton, 2014). Different interpretations about what constitutes child maltreatment also result in a variety of different explanations as to why children are abused and neglected.

In very simple terms child maltreatment can be defined as 'ways of treating children that are harmful or morally wrong' (Munro, 2007, p. 61). The World Health Organization (WHO) describes child maltreatment as including:

> ...all types of physical and/or emotional ill-treatment, sexual abuse, neglect, negligence and commercial or other exploitation, which results in actual or potential harm to the child's health, survival, development or dignity in the context of a relationship of responsibility, trust or power

(WHO, United Nations Office on Drugs and Crime and United Nations Development Programme, 2014, p. 82).

Exposure to domestic abuse is also recognised as a form of child maltreatment (WHO, United Nations Office on Drugs and Crime and United Nations Development Programme, 2014), alongside new and emerging forms of abuse such as female genital mutilation (FGM) and forced marriage.

These definitions also emphasise society's responsibilities and children's rights. An additional feature of child maltreatment is the focus on the life course and the negative impact that child abuse and neglect and other childhood adversity may have on long-term physical and mental health, educational and social outcomes later in life.

In the UK abuse and neglect are operationally defined in the statutory guidance. In the English guidance, *Working Together to Safeguard Children*, abuse is defined as:

> A form of maltreatment of a child. Somebody may abuse or neglect a child by inflicting harm, or by failing to act to prevent harm. Children may be abused in a family or in an institutional or community setting by those known to them or, more rarely, by others (e.g. via the internet). They may be abused by an adult or adults, or another child or children (HM Government, 2015, p. 92).

One of the main problems of working in the field of safeguarding and child protection is the difficulty of defining what is abuse and what is not. While some child maltreatment is very obvious – for example, severe incidents of physical abuse which result in permanent disability or death – some behaviour towards children is more difficult to classify as abuse or neglect, and to decide whether it is abuse or not (Kay, 1999).

Eileen Munro (2007, pp. 66–7) suggests that there are several reasons why it is very complex to apply such definitions in practice. These include: the diversity of parenting styles; difficulties in decisions about thresholds and what is 'good enough' parenting; and ambiguous evidence resulting in 'some degree of uncertainty', culpability and the problems associated with predicting actual harm and potential harm.

Safeguarding children and young people

In the UK and other countries with similar child protection systems, policies relating to risk and child protection focus broadly on responsibilities for safeguarding children and young people. Safeguarding, put simply, is concerned with 'keeping children safe from harm, such as illness, abuse or injury' (Children's Rights Director, 2004, p. 3). In the UK the term 'safeguarding' was originally referred to in the Children Act 1989, where a duty was placed on all local authorities 'to safeguard and promote the welfare' of children in need under Section 17. Introduced as the major piece of childcare legislation in the 1980s, the Children Act 1989 sought to achieve a balance around the rights and values of children and their parents, the nature of state intervention and the role of the family (Lawrence, 2004).

In England safeguarding and promoting the welfare of children is defined in the most recent version of the statutory guidance *Working Together to Safeguard Children* (HM Government, 2015) as:

- protecting children from maltreatment;
- preventing impairment of children's health or development;
- ensuring that children are growing up in circumstances consistent with the provision of safe and effective care;
- taking action to enable all children to have the best outcomes (HM Government 2015, p. 5).

The most recent version of this statutory guidance on child protection highlights a child-centred and co-ordinated approach to safeguarding (HM Government, 2015). This differs from the previous 2010 guidance, which had emphasised that safeguarding children's health and well-being was mainly achieved through good parenting. The new statutory guidance describes how effective safeguarding arrangements in local areas should be underpinned by two key principles:

- safeguarding is everyone's responsibility: for services to be effective each professional and organisation should play their full part;
- a child-centred approach: for services to be effective they should be based on a clear understanding of the needs and views of children (HM Government, 2015, p. 9).

Child protection

Child protection is defined in the statutory guidance *Working Together to Safeguard Children* as 'part of safeguarding and promoting welfare. This refers to the activity that is undertaken to protect specific children who are suffering, or are likely to suffer, significant harm' (HM Government, 2015, p. 92). Effective child protection is crucially important as part of wider work to safeguard and promote children's welfare. Since the 're-focusing debate' which followed publication of *Child Protection: Messages from Research* (DH, 1995) child protection has been accepted as a broad concept which includes all elements of children in need and significant harm.

Children in need

A child will be in need if his/her vulnerability is such that:

- he is unlikely to achieve or maintain, or have the opportunity of achieving or maintaining a reasonable standard of health or development without the provision for him of services by the local authority;
- his health or development is likely to be significantly impaired, or further impaired without the provision of such services; or
- he is disabled (Children Act, 1989, Part III, Sect 17(10)).

Children at risk of significant harm

'Significant harm' is the threshold beyond which 'children in need' are regarded as 'children in need of protection' and so child protection procedures are initiated. A child is in need of protection where there is likely or actual 'significant harm' to him/her or he/she is at risk. However the Children Act 1989 does not give a definitive interpretation of the concept of 'significant harm' (Appleton and Clemerson-Trew, 2008).

The relationship between safeguarding and child protection

The definitions above highlight a broad picture of safeguarding, which encompasses not only protection but also a broader and more positive emphasis on prevention and ensuring all children and young people's safety. The term 'safeguarding children' can therefore be regarded as 'an umbrella term [or spectrum] incorporating all aspects of work with vulnerable children, children in need and children who are suffering, or at risk of significant harm' (Appleton and Clemerson-Trew, 2008, p. 265).

Public health

Public health incorporates a number of key elements: it is population focused; preventative in nature; and multidisciplinary. The definition from the Faculty of Public Health draws attention to promotion, protection and prevention – describing public health as: 'The science and art of promoting and protecting health and well-being, preventing ill-health and prolonging life through the organised efforts of society' (Faculty of Public Health, 2010a).

The population focus means that public health is concerned with understanding and addressing health and disease within populations rather than just focusing upon the impact on individuals. Adopting a life-course approach to public health means targeting specific health challenges at different stages in a person's life: for example, by focusing on the promotion of early attachment during infancy; or by promoting sensible drinking behaviours among teenagers (DH and PHE, 2014). An important tool is epidemiology – this refers to the study of patterns, causes and effects of health and disease conditions in defined populations. Epidemiology has led to key insights about patterns of health and illness and in particular has drawn attention to inequalities which are now an important focus of public health work nationally and globally (Leon and Walt, 2000; Graham, 2009; DH, 2010; Marmot et al. 2010; Tod and Hirst, 2014).

Prevention can take place at different levels – primary, secondary and tertiary – and is informed by understanding risk factors and disease trajectories within an identified population. For example, interventions concerned with primary prevention focus upon preventing the problem occurring in the first place and include childhood immunisations and cervical screening programmes. Secondary prevention refers to interventions that prevent the disease or problem getting worse: for example, lifestyle changes for those with coronary heart disease or for those who are obese. Tertiary prevention describes activities that treat the symptoms of the disease or problem and which aim to mediate the outcome; examples of this include drug therapy to control pain for patients with life-limiting or chronic diseases such as cancer and rheumatoid arthritis. Thus preventative work refers to a wide range of interventions which vary according to the client population and the disease or problem being addressed.

Public health work is also multilayered and involves a wide range of activities and interventions. Shaped by public policy decisions – about for example the environment, taxation, housing and public service provision – public health work is undertaken by a variety of professionals, organisations, communities and individuals. Indeed multidisciplinary and collaborative working are key ingredients for successful public health work (Douglas, 2010). In the UK public health is informed by a range of policy and professional guidance (DH, 2010; Faculty of Public Health, 2010b; PHE, 2014) and constitutes a well-developed area of public policy, albeit one that often clashes with other political priorities. In England current public health priorities relating to children and young people include obesity, mental health and ensuring that every child has the best start in life (DH, 2013a; PHE, 2014). A pledge to improve the health outcomes of all children and young people and to reduce child deaths was made in 2013 (DH, 2013a). However public health is population and context specific and very different priorities are evident in low income countries where for example infections and malnutrition dominate the agenda (see Blair *et al.*, 2010).

Nevertheless both globally and nationally child maltreatment is now being understood within a public health framework (WHO, 2006; 2007; O'Donnell *et al.*, 2008; Gilbert *et al.*, 2009b; 2012; Barlow and Calam, 2011), and the reasons for this are discussed further in Chapter 2. Identification of child welfare needs, through services that are developed from sound public health principles, is of paramount importance for the well-being of all children in our society. Adopting a public health approach ensures that potentially vulnerable children can be identified early and that they receive the support and services that they and their families need to maximise the health and well-being of the child and potentially to prevent child maltreatment.

Legal and policy context

The government of each of the UK's four nations is responsible for child protection policy and practice. Each country has its own legislative framework. The Children Acts 1989 and 2004 are the key legislation for England and Wales. In Scotland the major legislation is the Children (Scotland) Act 1995 and in Northern Ireland it is the Children (Northern Ireland) Order 1995. Each nation also has its own statutory guidance: *Working Together to Safeguard Children* in England (HM Government, 2015); *Children and Young People: Rights to Action* (Welsh Assembly, 2004) and *All Wales Child Protection Procedures* (All Wales Child Protection Procedures Review Group, 2008) in Wales; *Getting It Right for Every Child* (Scottish Government, 2012) in Scotland; and *Cooperating to Safeguard Children* (DHSSPS, 2003) in Northern Ireland.

All nurses, midwives and health visitors working with children and their families have an important public health role in the identification of vulnerable children and children at risk of significant harm. All nursing staff must be trained and knowledgeable about the signs of child abuse and neglect. The English statutory guidance *Working Together to Safeguard Children* states that staff 'should receive training to ensure they attain the competences appropriate to their role and follow the relevant professional guidance' (HM Government, 2015, p. 56). This is mirrored in other statutory child protection guidance across Wales, Scotland and Northern Ireland.

The nationally recognised intercollegiate guidance (RCPCH, 2014) *Safeguarding Children and Young People: Roles and Competences for Healthcare Staff* has recently been revised, and this document outlines the competencies (including knowledge, skill, attitudes and values) required of all healthcare staff in relation to safeguarding children and young people, including education and training requirements. All healthcare organisations providing services for children must ensure that they have clear policies and procedures for employees about how to safeguard and promote the welfare of children (HM Government, 2015). In addition many nurses, midwives and health visitors will have access to practice guidance and both single-agency training through their organisations and multi-agency training through the Local Safeguarding Children Board (LSCB), which will aid in the identification of vulnerable children and young people. Nursing staff will also be supported by named and designated child protection professionals and by designated looked-after professionals.

Interestingly the latest truncated version of *Working Together to Safeguard Children* (HM Government, 2015) has removed much of the detail about the role of individual healthcare professionals who work with children in terms of safeguarding and identifying their welfare needs. Instead the guidance acknowledges that a range of healthcare staff play a very important role in child safeguarding. This is detailed as:

> ...understanding risk factors, communicating effectively with children and families, liaising with other agencies, assessing needs and capacity, responding to those needs and contributing to multi-agency assessments and reviews (HM Government, 2015, p. 56).

Nurses should be familiar with the clinical guideline *When to Suspect Child Maltreatment* (National Collaborating Centre for Women's and Children's Health, 2009) and Public Health England's National Child and Maternal Health Intelligence Network and the Safeguarding Knowledge Hub.

About this Book

This book developed from a series of papers which formed a symposium delivered at the International Society for the Prevention of Child Abuse & Neglect (ISPCAN) European Regional Conference held in Dublin in September 2013. The purpose of the symposium was to draw attention to the important contribution of nurses in protecting children from maltreatment; and to discuss this within a public health framework. The contributors are all experts within their field and the symposium generated considerable discussion and interest, largely because this topic has not been extensively addressed. Thus we hope *Child Protection, Public Health and Nursing* fills an important gap in the available literature on this topic and helps those working in the field or studying, managing and commissioning services to understand and appreciate the important contribution of the nursing workforce to the protection of children.

Indeed one of the themes within this book is the lack of research about the contribution of nurses to this area of work and their relative invisibility within the wider safeguarding children and public health policy field.

The book aims and content

Child Protection, Public Health and Nursing aims to highlight and critically examine nurses' contribution to protecting children from maltreatment. An organising theme throughout is public health, and this is addressed in different ways across all the chapters; in particular the nursing role in prevention, early identification and intervention are discussed. Given this orientation towards public health, the roles of specialist public health nurses such as health visitors and school nurses feature in many of the chapters, although the contribution of those who have more generic nursing roles but whose work brings them into contact with children, young people and their families are also considered.

The book is primarily focused upon policy and practice within the UK but material from an international context is also included, particularly in Chapter 4, which discusses comparative material from a wider European perspective. The chapters explore the inputs of nurses from different disciplines in their work in protecting children and young people. Throughout, the book draws on relevant theoretical, research and policy literature, but particularly focuses on the evidence base for practice.

In Chapter 2 Sue Peckover explains what is meant by a 'public health approach to child maltreatment and the implications of this for nursing'. Making reference to the wider literature on child maltreatment, it outlines what a public health approach entails and makes the case for adopting this in relation to child maltreatment. The argument for what is sometimes called an 'upstream' approach is shaped by what is known about the extent and impact of the problem, along with the crisis in protective services to respond. Central to this shift is concern for the welfare of children and young people – and thus the argument for prevention and early intervention is persuasive. The chapter also outlines the important role that nurses have in prevention and early identification work with children, young people and their families. Here the focus is upon UK policy and practice with some of the key attributes illustrated by a short discussion of school nursing.

The contribution of health visiting to child protection practice is the focus of Chapter 3, written by Jane Appleton. The British health visiting service has been established for more than 150 years and provides a universal and public health preventative service to all preschool children and their families. A distinctive aspect of the health visitors' role is that these public health professionals make home visits to all children and their families, and they are therefore in a unique position to identify vulnerable families and children at risk of abuse and neglect. This chapter explores the health visitor's role in safeguarding and child protection work through an analysis of research evidence and recent policy directives, such as the English *Health Visitor Implementation Plan* (DH, 2011) and new 4–5–6 service model (DH, 2014a). The chapter concludes by emphasising that health visitors' work in child protection should be viewed as a continuum of public health activity including universal preventative work, targeting services according to need, identifying and working with vulnerable children and their families, and protecting children from abuse and neglect.

Chapter 4 adopts an international perspective as Caroline Bradbury-Jones, Eija Paavilainen and Julie Taylor report on a rapid appraisal of public health nursing practice in relation to child protection from a pan-European perspective. The chapter highlights areas of interesting and innovative practice from individual countries, as well as variations and similarities in practice – with Finland used as a more focused example of how this area of work is developing. The scoping exercise highlights the similarities that exist across some countries such as Scandinavia and the UK, and also shows that other countries have limited scope for public health nurses in a child protection capacity. Summarising these nuanced differences is important in gauging the extent to which different countries recognise the crucial role that public health nurses can play in the support and surveillance of children up to age five or six. This chapter captures the current knowledge base about the specific child protection remit of public health nurses across the EU (European Union) and how this is enacted and supported and provides some useful insights beyond those previously available.

In Chapter 5 Catherine Powell outlines the contribution of the wider nursing and midwifery workforce in ensuring the safety and well-being of children and young people. The chapter begins by highlighting the practice, policy and professional guidance that provide the mandate for a whole profession responsibility to embed a proactive and responsive approach to the prevention of child maltreatment and the recognition and referral of child protection concerns. It then moves on to consider examples from practice which reflect the healthcare journeys that may be experienced by children, young people and their families. This chapter considers the opportunities that may be presented within these contexts for more proactive and responsive safeguarding children practice across the wider nursing profession.

In Chapter 6 Caroline Bradbury-Jones and Julie Taylor focus specifically on the role of public health nurses in identifying and responding to children where safeguarding is an issue. The importance of early detection and intervention is widely accepted. In most instances however the alerting factors are not clear or sudden, but vague, cumulative and insidious, which make detection and early intervention problematic. This chapter will draw upon two research studies – one on dental neglect, the other on domestic abuse – to show the complexities associated with public health nurses' safeguarding decision-making. The authors outline some of the barriers and challenges associated with their assessments and the tentative steps they take in weighing up the small signs and big risks. While public health nurses play a crucial safeguarding role, this chapter highlights the multiplicity of interrelated contextual factors that might compound early detection and intervention, including risks to children and a need to protect future contacts.

The focus of Chapter 7 by Suzanne Smith is on leadership in child protection for safeguarding children and adult leads within the context of the acute general hospital setting. This chapter draws on the author's current role and expertise as Head of Safeguarding in an NHS acute trust and examines some of the important issues facing current safeguarding leadership from both a nursing and wider healthcare perspective. Changes to commissioning and provider arrangements have brought a change to the location and development of safeguarding lead roles including statutory named and designated roles and emergent non-statutory positions. These changes present a challenge to the potential for safeguarding leads to remain clinically connected. Within the acute sector, the visibility of safeguarding is a constant challenge with a real and apparent disconnect between safeguarding and the patient safety and quality agendas, and a focus on technical solutions and knowledge frameworks which do not easily lend themselves to safeguarding practice. The chapter argues that in acute care organisations the safeguarding children and adult strategy should be strategically located throughout the three key domains of quality including patient safety, patient experience and clinical effectiveness from the objectives of the safeguarding team through to the corporate objectives of the board.

The final chapter draws together key themes emerging from the discussion of child protection, public health and nursing in the six main chapters. In this, we (Jane Appleton and Sue Peckover) argue that the adoption of a public health approach is not without tensions. We discuss the socially constructed nature of child abuse and neglect, and provide some critical perspectives upon public health, current policy and their implications for nurses. The visibility of the nursing contribution to safeguarding children is also highlighted. Discussion of key themes includes gaps in the evidence base and the need for further research to inform policy and practice about the nursing contribution to protecting children and young people.

To conclude, we hope this book will be of interest to all qualified nurses working in acute care and primary care settings who have contact with children, young people and their families. It will also be relevant to those undertaking post-qualifying and postgraduate courses from all branches of nursing and midwifery who need to be aware of their duties in protecting children and young people.

Conclusion

As frontline healthcare professionals, nurses, midwives and health visitors have a key role to play in the prevention of child abuse and neglect and in the protection of children and young people. This introductory chapter has provided a brief overview of key terms including public health, child protection, safeguarding and other related concepts which will be examined in greater detail in relation to nursing practice in the following chapters.

CHAPTER 2

Child maltreatment: An issue for public health nursing

Sue Peckover, Sheffield Hallam University

Introduction

This chapter will provide an overview of why child maltreatment is a public health issue. It will discuss the key elements of a public health approach and explain why there has been a shift in thinking towards adopting this as a means to tackle child maltreatment. The chapter will also draw attention to the important role played by nurses in public health who are well placed to work with children and young people and their families and undertake preventative and early intervention work; their role and contribution will be examined, drawing upon some examples from UK policy and practice.

What is child maltreatment?

As outlined in the introductory chapter the concept of child maltreatment poses difficulties in relation to terminology and definitions. The following wording for child maltreatment is used by the WHO and provides a useful framework for understanding the issues addressed in this chapter. It defines child maltreatment as:

> ...all forms of physical and/or emotional ill-treatment, sexual abuse, neglect or negligent treatment or commercial or other exploitation, resulting in actual or potential harm to the child's health, survival, development or dignity in the context of a relationship of responsibility, trust or power (WHO, 2006, p. 9).

In this chapter this terminology of child maltreatment will be used, although many authors and policies adopt other interchangeable terms such as 'child abuse and neglect'.

Why is child maltreatment a public health issue?

Understanding child maltreatment as a public health issue reflects a significant shift in thinking about how this topic is conceptualised and addressed. Reasons for this include the extent of the problem, the impact and costs of child maltreatment, and the importance of early intervention for children's well-being (Barlow and Calam, 2011; Gilbert *et al.*, 2012).

The extent of child maltreatment

In recent years researchers have attempted to estimate how many children and young people are maltreated (Gilbert *et al.*, 2009a; Radford *et al.*, 2011; 2013). Although this has created some methodological challenges because of the different ways child maltreatment is defined and understood, the overall results provide an important indication of the extent to which children and young people experience maltreatment or abuse during childhood. For example the review conducted by Gilbert *et al.* (2009a), which draws upon data from a number of retrospective population-based surveys, suggests about 10% of children under eighteen years of age experience abuse and neglect each year. Similarly findings from a UK prevalence study undertaken by the NSPCC found large numbers of children, young people and young adults had experienced maltreatment (see Table 2.1) (Radford *et al.* 2011; 2013).

Table 2.1 Findings from NSPCC prevalence study of child maltreatment.

Abuse reported	under 11 years (n=2,160)*	11–17 year olds (n=2,275)**	18–24 years (n=1,761)
'severe maltreatment'§	5.9%	18.6%	25.3%
'maltreatment' by a parent or guardian during their childhood	5%	13.4%	14.5%

Source: Radford *et al.*, 2011

* parents or guardians

** plus additional information provided by parents or guardians

§ 'severe maltreatment' included severe physical and emotional abuse by adults, severe neglect by parents or guardians and contact sexual abuse.

The NSPCC study also found that females reported higher rates than males (Radford *et al.*, 2011, p. 8), and that multiple forms of abuse were widely reported. While these findings represent retrospective views they are based on a large random sample and broadly reflect findings from a similar earlier study (Cawson *et al.*, 2000).

These population-based, self-report studies have made an important contribution to our knowledge base about child maltreatment. In particular they demonstrate the range of severity of children's experiences of maltreatment. As Gilbert *et al.*, (2012) point out:

> child maltreatment involves a range of severity that reaches far into the 'normal' population. Maltreatment is not inflicted only by unimaginably vicious or neglectful parents but occurs as part of a spectrum of parenting behaviour ranging from optimal to severely abusive (Gilbert *et al.*, 2012, p. 326).

This has implications for interventions, particularly those concerned with improving parenting (see Barlow and Calam, 2011), and is addressed later in this chapter.

Another important contribution of these studies is that they demonstrate child maltreatment is much more extensive than the number of 'known' cases may suggest. For example population-based, self-report studies indicate 4–10% of children in the UK experience child maltreatment each year, compared to the 1% of the population known to child protection agencies (Gilbert *et al.*, 2009a; Radford *et al.*, 2011). There are a number of reasons that children are not known to child protection agencies: for example, minimisation and concealment of the abuse; lack of detection; and under-reporting (Gilbert *et al.*, 2009a). Nevertheless there remains a wide gap between self-reported rates and known cases. This implies that cases known to child protection agencies only represent the 'tip of the iceberg' of child maltreatment, with a high level of unmet need in the general population of children and young people (Radford *et al.*, 2013, p. 810).

Thus emerging knowledge – which has highlighted the range of severity and extent of child maltreatment within the wider population – supports the adoption of a proactive public health approach in addressing this problem. This is further supported by knowledge of the impact of child maltreatment considered in the next section.

The impact of child maltreatment

Experiencing child maltreatment has a number of adverse consequences, impacting in the short and/or long term on physical and mental health, social and economic functioning and general well-being (Corso *et al.*, 2008; Gilbert *et al.*, 2009b; Radford *et al.*, 2011). The impact of child maltreatment on individuals varies considerably and is not fully understood. It of course depends upon a number of factors including the type and severity of the abuse, the context in which it occurs and the wider risk and protective factors. However the main pathways leading to adverse consequences have been identified (see Meadows *et al.*, 2011); these are due to:

- physical changes in the developing brain as a consequence of stress or trauma;
- difficulties in forming and maintaining relationships;
- mental health-related responses to stress and trauma;
- the development of adult behaviour patterns based on those observed at home;
- disruption to education and social relationships caused by family disruption due to maltreatment.

These provide a useful framework for understanding the multiple adverse consequences of child maltreatment. That they can be serious and insidious are best illustrated by a large Californian study which found that adults who had experienced adverse childhood experiences such as psychological, physical and sexual abuse experienced poorer health and well-being and were more likely to adopt risk-taking behaviour such as smoking and drinking (Felitti *et al.*, 1998; Corso *et al.*, 2008; Brown *et al.*, 2009). Known as the Adverse Childhood Experiences (ACE) study, this large-scale survey completed by 9,508 adults provides clear evidence of the longer-term impacts of child abuse and neglect. More recent research details further evidence that experiencing childhood maltreatment contributes to adult health problems (Min *et al.*, 2013).

The costs of child maltreatment

As well as having adverse consequences for individuals, child maltreatment also incurs a range of wider costs for public services, the economy and society. These occur at different points in time and include additional costs to health, education, children's services and the criminal justice system, as well as reduced productivity and unemployment (see for example Segal and Dalziel, 2011; Fang *et al.*, 2012; Saied-Tessier, 2014). It is hard to estimate with accuracy the economic costs of child maltreatment but attempts to do so suggest they are significant. For example Fang *et al.* (2012) estimate the economic burden of child maltreatment in the US to be approximately $124 billion for 2008. In the UK the prevalence cost of child sexual abuse has been estimated as £3.2 billion for 2012 (Saied-Tessier, 2014). It is also evident that across the developed world child protective services are overwhelmed with workload and struggling to respond to known cases where children require protection from abuse (see Jütte *et al.*, 2014). Similarly mental health support for children and young people who have experienced abuse and require tertiary level interventions to help them adapt or recover from their experiences is lacking (see Eastman, 2014). This is not only problematic in terms of delivering appropriate and timely interventions to protect and support children and young people affected by child maltreatment, but it is also costly. As Fang *et al.* (2012) argue:

> Compared with other health problems, the burden of child maltreatment is substantial, indicating the importance of prevention efforts to address the high prevalence of child maltreatment (Fang *et al.*, 2012, p. 156).

The implication underpinning an economic perspective on child maltreatment is that investment aimed at prevention and early intervention translates into later savings. This is a persuasive argument for policymakers concerned with scarce public resources – and provides another important reason for adopting a public health approach to address child maltreatment.

Towards a public health approach: 'Risk' and 'early intervention'

Understanding the extent and range of severity of child maltreatment, as well as its costs and impacts, all point towards the value of adopting a public health approach (Barlow and Calam, 2011; Daniel *et al.*, 2011, pp. 143–60; Gilbert *et al.*, 2012). As outlined above this is population focused and oriented towards prevention and early intervention; it also aims to reduce risk factors associated with child maltreatment (Gilbert *et al.*, 2012). While a detailed discussion of these is beyond the scope of this chapter the social ecological framework (Bronfenbrenner, 1979) provides a useful basis for understanding both risk and protective factors for child maltreatment. These include: environmental and community factors such as housing, social support and resources; parental/carer factors such as parental mental and physical health, domestic abuse, substance use and overall parenting capacity; and factors relating to the child/young person such as developmental age and ability, health and behaviour (Bronfenbrenner, 1979; Gilbert *et al.*, 2012). These risk factors are however broad in scope and do create challenges for designing policy and practice to prevent child maltreatment, and in particular for identifying the focus of interventions and attributing clear outcomes in order to demonstrate effectiveness (see MacMillan *et al.*, 2009).

Nevertheless there remains wide scope for developing public health approaches to addressing child maltreatment, and a shift in focus is evident in policy responses globally and nationally. Public health is central to the strategic direction adopted by the WHO to address child maltreatment; this is systematic and multi-sectoral and incorporates primary, secondary and tertiary prevention strategies (WHO, 2006; 2007). In the UK a public health approach to tackling sexual abuse has been outlined by the NSPCC (Brown *et al.*, 2011). It is also possible to identify a shift in focus in the earlier *Every Child Matters* reforms, which introduced a broad remit for promoting the safety and welfare of all children in England (Chief Secretary to the Treasury, 2003). Central to this was early intervention, which continues as a key theme in public policy concerned with the early years and child protection (Allen, 2011a; Munro, 2011; Tickell, 2011; Scottish Government, 2012).

Early intervention refers to any intervention delivered in a timely manner before things start to go wrong or get worse. Examples include parenting support to improve the provision of basic care for a child, promote attachment or support better behaviour management. Such interventions can be delivered through parenting or home-visiting programmes such as the Family Nurse Partnership or the Triple P Programme (MacMillan *et al.*, 2009; Moullin *et al.*, 2014). Indeed, MacMillan *et al.* (2009) found that these types of targeted interventions to help prevent child maltreatment can be better and more cost-effective than interventions to protect children once maltreatment has occurred. Moreover some have argued that the range of severity of child maltreatment identified in self-report studies (discussed above) indicates that a broad spectrum of parenting behaviour exists within the general population and for this to be addressed requires universal parenting support strategies; this will improve parenting overall and contribute to reducing child maltreatment (Barlow and Calam, 2011; Daniel *et al.*, 2011, pp. 143–60; Gilbert *et al.*, 2012, p. 328).

In the UK the focus upon early intervention is currently oriented towards improving parenting particularly for families where children are under three years old. This is a key theme of public policy and informed by neuroscientific evidence about the quality of parenting, attachment and its impact upon brain development (see Allen, 2011a; Cuthbert *et al.*, 2011; Tickell, 2011; WAVE Trust, 2013; Moullin *et al.*, 2014; Macvarish *et al.*, 2014). Importantly it identifies the early years as a critical period in a child's life when experiencing adversity such as poor parenting and attachment cannot later be mitigated if circumstances improve. This life-course perspective creates an additional argument for adopting a public health preventative and early intervention approach to addressing child maltreatment (see for example Blair *et al.*, 2010).

Thus in this context 'early intervention' also has a temporal component referring as it does to a child's age and development. This is sometimes referred to as the 'child's time frame' and is becoming a particularly prominent concept in child protection work (Brown and Ward, 2013). It involves ensuring interventions are delivered in a timely manner for children and young people in order to prevent or avoid prolonged exposure to child maltreatment or adverse experiences such as poor parenting. It also recognises that delayed or late interventions may leave children exposed for a longer period of time at crucial stages in their development. This life-course perspective on child maltreatment provides an additional argument for adopting a public health approach to addressing the problem and is apparent at secondary and tertiary levels as well as in primary prevention (Blair *et al.*, 2010).

While strategies to support and strengthen parenting are highly evident in current UK children's policy (Macvarish *et al.*, 2014) there are many other examples of early intervention measures designed to address child maltreatment (MacMillan *et al.*, 2009; Munro, 2011). These include: targeted support services for women and children affected by domestic abuse (see for example Ramsay *et al.*, 2009; Spinney, 2013); school-based preventative programmes (see Alexander *et al.*, 2005); and awareness-raising campaigns such as those run by the NSPCC and other children's charities to highlight key topics such as teenage partner abuse or child neglect. Examples of 'early intervention' in relation to child maltreatment will of course vary according to the issue being addressed and whether it is part of a universal preventative strategy or a targeted intervention for an individual child, young person or family; they may also be delivered by a range of professionals and agencies working separately or collaboratively as part of a preventative public health approach to address child maltreatment. This will include measures delivered by public health nurses who work with children, young people and their families (see Powell, 2007; 2011; Watson and Rodwell, 2014). Their role and contribution are outlined in the next section and discussed further in later chapters of this book.

The role of public health nurses in the UK

There are a number of different public health nursing roles in the UK. These include specialist community public health nurses (SCPHN) such as school nurses, health visitors and community children's nurses who undertake specific public health nursing roles with children and families (Cowley, 2008; DH, 2009a). Public health also forms part of the role of general practice nurses and midwives. There are also a number of specialist nursing roles which focus upon the needs of vulnerable groups such as looked-after children, asylum seekers and homeless people, and this work by definition incorporates a public health orientation (see Cowley, 2008; Watkins and Cousins, 2010; Linsley *et al.*, 2011). In England public health nurses are also involved in delivering the Family Nurse Partnership, an effective early intervention parenting programme offered to teenage mothers from pregnancy until their child reaches the age of two years (MacMillan *et al.*, 2009). In addition every NHS (National Health Service) Trust and organisation is required to employ specialist nurses with particular responsibilities for safeguarding children and young people. The remit of the named and designated nurses is to provide strategic direction and support, training or supervision for frontline professionals, and as such they make an important public health contribution to safeguarding children (Appleton, 2012; HM Government, 2015; NHS Commissioning Board, 2013; RCPCH, 2014).

Public health nursing takes place in a wide range of settings; these include schools, children centres and clinics and (particularly for health visitors and community paediatric nurses) involves home visiting (Cowley, 1995; Cowley, *et al.*, 2013). Importantly all public health nurses work with other agencies and professionals as well as with children, families and communities (Cowley, 2008; Watkins and Cousins, 2010; Linsley *et al.*, 2011). In England health visitors and school nurses lead and deliver the Healthy Child Programme (HCP). This covers the population aged 0–19 years and is offered on a progressive universal basis; this means that all families receive a universal service with additional support available for those with specific needs and risks (DH, 2009a; 2009b). Thus health visitors and school nurses are particularly well placed to contribute to the early identification and prevention of child maltreatment (Appleton, 2011; Powell, 2007; 2011; Watson and Rodwell, 2014). This is because their work brings them into contact with children and families across the population and with whom they have a continuing relationship. This has been somewhat challenged in recent years with large caseloads and more limited universal service provision, although recent investment in health visiting in England has strengthened the service (DH, 2011). Nonetheless the nature

of public health nursing work means that they know their clients –
just like others working in primary care such as GPs (Appleton and
Cowley, 2008a; Woodman *et al.*, 2014). This knowledge is important in assessing changing needs and risks and in offering a historical perspective upon changes in a child or young person's life
course (Powell, 2007; 2011). Public health nurses also operate with a
holistic concept of 'health', which incorporates social, emotional and
physical well-being, rather than focusing just upon illness or disease
(Cowley, 2008; Watkins and Cousins, 2010; Linsley *et al.*, 2011). This
enables them to understand the broader context in which families
and children live and the impacts of this upon health, well-being
and safety. As these include understandings of the community and
environment as well as parenting, social and family relationships,
public health nurses are very well placed to identify and address risk
factors for child maltreatment (Bronfenbrenner, 1979; Powell, 2007;
2011; Gilbert *et al.*, 2012).

The varied nature of public health nursing roles make it hard to
describe their activities although Table 2.2 provides an overview of
some key features.

Table 2.2 An action summary for public health nursing work.

Public health nursing involves ...	
visiting	measuring
talking	weighing
identifying	immunising
observing	befriending
monitoring	recording
reassuring	prescribing
signposting	empowering
referring	gatekeeping
supporting	advising

These verbs indicate the action orientation of public health
nursing work. As such it could be argued that public health nurses
have an important role to play as 'eyes' and 'ears' in detecting and
responding at an early stage to children and young people at risk
of, or experiencing maltreatment (Powell, 2007; 2011; Watson and
Rodwell, 2014). In order to illustrate this further the next section
outlines the role of school nurses.

School nurses

School nurses undertake an important role in relation to the pre-vention, identification and early intervention of child maltreat-ment. They work specifically with children within the school-age population and often have responsibility for particular schools. As part of their role they undertake health needs assessments for the school population as a whole, and for the individual children and young people they work with. A key feature of this aspect of their work is their community knowledge; this includes understand-ing socio-economic and environmental factors shaping the health, well-being and safety of the school population. School nurses also have an understanding of relevant children's public health issues and inequalities and will use the health needs assessment pro-cesses to plan and deliver services at both individual and school level (see for example De Bell, 2007).

School nursing work is varied and incorporates a range of approaches and strategies. These include: individual health reviews; drop-in clinics for children and young people to access support voluntarily; and the provision of educational and health promotion resources for individual children and young people, or for classes or schools. They also undertake home visits and work with parents and/or carers as well as undertaking a wide range of liaison and multi-agency work across the wider health and social care environment. School nurses utilise a variety of skills and techniques in their work such as strength-based approaches and motivational interviewing. Because they provide an important link between home and school, they are particularly well placed to deliver a range of interventions which strengthen parenting and address behaviour and emotional health and well-being (see for example Day, 2005; Kelly *et al.*, 2005).

Clearly the range of issues facing school nurses in their work with children and young people is broad and depends upon the particular populations they are working with. However their work is likely to include a variety of activities concerned with the moni-toring, promotion and protection of children and young people's physical, emotional and sexual health. The promotion of healthy lifestyles – particularly focusing upon key health issues such as diet, drugs and smoking – is an important element of school nursing work, as is a growing range of sexual health work (Lane and Day, 2001; Brown, 2012).

School nurses also contribute to the support of parenting both through individual work and via the delivery of specific parenting programmes (see for example Day, 2005). In addition school nurses will play a role in the support, liaison and integration of children and young people who have additional health needs and disabilities including emotional issues (Kelly *et al.*, 2005). They also of course have an important specific role in safeguarding children and young people by identifying, addressing and referring children and young people affected by issues such as neglect, child sexual abuse and exploitation, and domestic violence (Clarke, 2000; Hackett, 2013). Thus school nurses are ideally placed to make an important public health contribution to addressing child maltreatment (Appleton, in press; Powell, 2007; 2011).

Public health nurses and child maltreatment
While public health nurses make an important contribution to addressing child maltreatment through prevention, early intervention and input into formal child safeguarding arrangements (Powell, 2007; 2011; Watson and Rodwell, 2014), there is surprisingly limited research that specifically examines this aspect of their role. This point was raised in a recent review of health visiting research undertaken by Cowley *et al.* (2013), but the paucity is also evident across the other public health nursing roles. The few relevant studies have focused for example upon professional assessment of vulnerability (see for example Appleton, 1996), domestic abuse (Frost, 1999; Peckover, 2002) and supervision (Lister and Crisp, 2005; Hall, 2007; Bradbury-Jones, 2013), although discussion of public health nursing roles in protecting children and the need for support is evident in the literature (see for example Clarke, 2000; Crisp and Lister, 2004; Marcellus, 2005; Appleton, 2011; Kent *et al.*, 2011; Hackett, 2013; Peckover, 2013). To some extent this limited research base in relation to child maltreatment reflects the breadth of the role undertaken by public health nurses with families and children and the challenges in

attributing outcomes to public health nursing roles (Elkan *et al.*, 2000). Nevertheless it is problematic as it means that the important role and contribution of public health nursing to the prevention, identification and addressing of child maltreatment remains hidden (Cowley *et al.*, 2013).

Conclusion

Knowledge about the extent, impact and costs of child maltreatment outlined in this chapter provide a very clear rationale for adopting a public health approach to address the problem. This involves understanding patterns and prevalence of problems within a population and responding to need through early identification and preventative activities. As outlined above, the public health nurse's role brings them into contact with the whole population of children and families, and their work is oriented towards prevention and early intervention. This make them very well placed to contribute to addressing child maltreatment through a public health approach – and this aspect of their role is further explored in the following chapters of this book.

CHAPTER 3

The unique contribution of British health visiting to child protection practice[1]

Jane V. Appleton, Oxford Brookes University

Introduction

This chapter explores the contribution of British health visiting to child protection practice. The British health visiting service, which was first established more than 150 years ago, provides a universal and public health preventative service to all preschool children and their families. A key feature of the health visitors' role is that these public health professionals make home visits to all children and their families, which has meant that the service is viewed as acceptable by parents and available to all. Health visitors are in a unique position to provide a targeted service according to need, to work with vulnerable families to build resilience and to identify children at risk of abuse and neglect. The chapter begins with a brief overview of the role of the health visitor historically and in contemporary society, outlining the services that health visitors deliver to children and families. It then moves on to explore health visiting's track record in safeguarding and child protection and draws on key research evidence, recent policy drivers and contemporary developments in health visiting such as the English Department of Health's 2011–2015 *Health Visitor Implementation Plan* (DH, 2011) and new service delivery model (DH, 2014a; 2014b). The chapter concludes by emphasising the distinctive contribution of health visitors' work in child protection practice, acknowledging that this should be part of a continuum of public health activity including universal preventative work, identifying and working with vulnerable children and their families, as well as protecting children from abuse and neglect.

Background

In 2012 health visiting celebrated its 150th anniversary. This service has its origins in public health, having developed within the philanthropic sanitary reform movements in the mid-nineteenth century (Cowley and Appleton, 2000). 'Sanitary visitor' was the original name for a health visitor, and they would visit local communities to improve environmental and public health (Owen, 1977, p. 5). The key priorities at that time were to reduce infectious diseases and improve sanitation (Adams, 2012). At the beginning of the twentieth century 'there was a growing sense of public concern about high infant mortality rates', and following the 1907 Notification of Births Act it became compulsory in 1915 to report new births across England (Owen, 1977, p. 8). This provided the health visitor with information about the babies born in their local communities, and it created opportunities to gain access to homes and offer guidance on infant management (Owen, 1977).

Health visiting today continues to be a public health, preventative service centred mainly on improving child and family health and reducing health inequalities (Adams, 2012; DH, 2014a; Scottish Government, 2011; 2012). A unique aspect of the health visitor's role is that these professionals make home visits (Adams, 2012) to all children and families, so it is a universal service targeted according to need (Cowley *et al.*, 2013; 2014). This has meant that the service is largely viewed as non-stigmatising and supportive (Donetto *et al.*, 2013), although some authors have examined the 'surveillance' aspects of the role (Bloor and McIntosh, 1990; Peckover, 2002). In a recent briefing for local government, NICE (2014a, p. 3) stresses that health visiting 'is valued and accepted by parents' and provides an important 'opportunity to give support and advice to parents and promote positive parenting, emotional attachment and bonding'.

Contemporary Health Visiting

A health visitor is a qualified nurse or midwife who has undertaken a further one-year, full-time or two-year, part-time, post-registration SCPHN course, studying at graduate or postgraduate level to gain further training, education and expertise in child and family health, health promotion and public health. The majority of health visitors work in the community as part of a primary healthcare team, assessing the health needs of individuals, families and the wider community. The health visiting team may include healthcare assistants, nursery nurses and other specialist health professionals (NICE, 2014a).

Health visitors' work begins during pregnancy in the transition to parenthood. Their role primarily involves supporting new parents and preschool children, providing expert advice, evidence-based support and interventions (NHS England, 2014).

Health visiting is underpinned by four principles that guide and direct professional practice. These are: the search for health needs; creating awareness of health needs; influencing policies affecting health; and the facilitation of health-enhancing activities (CETHV, 1977; Cowley and Frost, 2006). In England the service is based on a 4–5–6 model which is discussed later in the chapter (DH, 2014a).

Aspects of the health visitor role include:

- Leading the local delivery of the HCP (DH, 2009a), which is underpinned by an evidence base (PHE, 2015). The HCP is the early intervention and prevention public health programme which is offered to every child and family across England and includes a programme of screening tests, immunisations, health and developmental reviews and guidance to support parenting, healthy choices and to promote social and emotional development and behaviour change. The programme provides support from early pregnancy to an infant's early weeks and throughout their childhood, providing opportunities for professionals to identify needs and deliver appropriate interventions (NICE, 2014a), as well as referring or directing on to other services when required.
- Advising new parents on aspects of parenting such as infant feeding, sleeping, weaning, child safety, immunisation and promoting their baby's physical and emotional development. Health visitors also provide practical help and advice to promote good health and prevent illness.
- Adopting a life-course approach to public health. Health visitors work with children and families to mitigate risk factors and build coping skills (PHE, 2014).
- Empowering parents to make decisions about their family's health and well-being. Health visitors work in partnership

with parents to develop and agree individualised health plans to address parenting and child/family health needs.

- Managing child health clinics in GP practices, community and Sure Start children centres and running specialist group sessions on: home safety; baby massage; healthy eating/infant weaning; exercise; and child development.
- Taking a central role in tackling and reducing inequalities and improving the health outcomes of populations (NHS England, 2014). As public health professionals, health visitors 'contribute to health needs analysis using tools such as the Early Years Profiles' (NHS England, 2014, p. 6).
- Playing a key role in identifying and working with vulnerable children and families with complex needs, particularly around issues to do with postnatal depression and domestic violence, adult mental health, alcohol or substance misuse. As part of tackling the impact of social inequality on health, health visitors work closely with deprived groups or those at risk of poorer outcomes to help them make use of available services (Marmot *et al.*, 2010). Increasingly social networking communication is used to enhance the service offer and access hard-to-reach groups.

It is worth noting that there are variations in the health visitor role in Scotland, Wales and Northern Ireland. However the underpinning principle of working to improve population health remains the same in all countries.

Health visiting, safeguarding children and child protection

As health visitors have a key preventive role, working primarily to support new parents and preschool children, they have an important responsibility for safeguarding and protecting children too. Safeguarding children is a public health priority, and includes both child protection and the prevention of harm to babies and children (NHS England, 2014). Safeguarding and promoting the welfare of children are defined in the English statutory child protection guidance *Working Together to Safeguard Children* (HM Government, 2015) as:

- protecting children from maltreatment;
- preventing impairment of children's health or development;

- ensuring that children are growing up in circumstances consistent with the provision of safe and effective care;
- taking action to enable all children to have the best outcomes (HM Government, 2015, p. 5).

This definition of safeguarding not only covers protection and safety issues but also gives a broader and more positive focus on prevention and ensuring all children and young people's well-being. Safeguarding includes many preventative activities which are included in the health visitors' domain such as protection from disease through immunisation, preventing impairment of children's emotional health and development, promoting healthy weight and nutrition, and reducing accidents as well as protecting children from child abuse and neglect. Effective child protection must be viewed as part of broader work to safeguard and promote the welfare of children (HM Government, 2015), and certainly health visitors do have an established track record in safeguarding and child protection work (HVA, 1994; Rouse, 2002; Appleton, 2011; Peckover, 2013).

Recent research on health visiting and child protection

So what does the research evidence tell us about the health visitors' contribution to child protection? In terms of the client group, evidence from the national survey of health visitor activities conducted by Cowley *et al.* (2007) found health visitors had most frequent contact with babies under one year old, closely followed by preschool children. This is important from a child protection perspective as SCRs continually identify that the greatest risks to children is when they are younger than one year of age (Cuthbert *et al.*, 2011). In terms of prevention, intervening early to support parenting is crucially important in addressing infant development and in promoting secure attachment and bonding (APPG, 2015; PHE, 2015). Yet there are still only a few research studies that have specifically examined health visitors' work in safeguarding and child protection (Appleton, 1996; Ling and Luker, 2000; Crisp and Lister, 2004; Coles and Collins, 2007; Cowley *et al.*, 2013), although some research on aspects of child protection work has focused on and/or involved health visitors, alongside other professionals (e.g. Appleton, 2012; Peckover and Trotter, 2014).

Most of the preventive work carried out by health visitors involves an element of safeguarding, and their key role in child protection is in identifying (or case-finding) children who are at risk of experiencing significant harm, and then initiating formal child protection procedures through referral to children's social care services. My own research with health visitors (Appleton, 1996) found that health visitors had four key yet diverse roles to play with vulnerable families. These included: identification of vulnerability, support agent, referral agent, and reluctant monitor. Health visitors were often very concerned about those children who they identified as highly vulnerable but where there was no involvement from children's social care services (Appleton, 1996).

Longitudinal research studies that have looked at health visitor screening for risk factors in a single postnatal assessment have not helped accurately to identify those families who would go on to abuse/maltreat a child (Browne and Saqi, 1988; Appleton, 1994; Browne, 1995; Dixon *et al.*, 2009; Cowley *et al.*, 2013). This therefore indicates that home visits and contacts as part of a universal service are important. Indeed Barlow *et al.*'s (2007) study of intensive home visiting suggested that, while there was no significant difference in the incidence of child abuse and neglect between the two study groups, child maltreatment could have been picked up early because the health visitors were making more frequent home visits.

Research examining health visitors' professional judgements has found that health visitors prioritise families on their caseloads according to key risk factors, while also taking into account context and family strengths. This process is dynamic and multi-factorial, requiring repeated assessments and awareness of the whole context, and focuses on seven critical attributes of needs assessment practice. These include:

- holistic assessment;
- assessment as a complex and multi-factorial process;
- ongoing nature of assessment;
- taking account of difficult-to-articulate issues;
- influence of practitioners' personal values and life experience;
- recognition that all clients can potentially have unmet needs;
- prioritisation (Appleton and Cowley, 2008a; 2008b).

Other research shows that in the 1990s there was a preoccupation by NHS managers with needs assessment tools, structured guidance and protocols as NHS managers increasingly required health visitors to identify vulnerable children and families using such tools. However research shows that these are largely unhelpful and are inadequate in measuring families' requirements (Appleton and Cowley, 2004). Such needs assessment tools do not improve identification of risk (Barlow *et al.*, 2012), and may even through insensitive questioning (Cowley and Houston, 2003) and mechanistic practices (Mitcheson and Cowley, 2003) inhibit relationship formation and trust, thereby alienating and reducing access by the families who need services the most (Appleton and Cowley, 2004).

More recently the Scottish Starting Well project has provided evidence that those vulnerable families needing most input were not consistently identified by health visitors as high risk in their baby's first four months of life using a family needs score and health plan (Wright *et al.*, 2009). These researchers argue that certainly in deprived areas a majority of families require continued health visiting input 'if the most vulnerable families are to be reliably identified' (Wright *et al.*, 2009, p. 23). This view is reinforced by Wilson *et al.* (2011, p. 6), who found that maternal depression scores measured at thirteen-month health visitor home visits 'acted as an additional powerful indicator of need'. These researchers concluded that a routine visit focusing on difficulties in parenting at thirteen months may be important in identifying families requiring additional support.

Learning from Serious Case Reviews

The value of universal provision of health visiting services is further reinforced in the common themes emerging from reviews of SCRs (known as significant case reviews in Scotland, child practice reviews in Wales and case management reviews in Northern Ireland). A number of biennial reviews by Brandon and colleagues have analysed common themes from SCRs, and these draw attention to the fact that many cases concern babies under one year of age (Brandon *et al.*, 2008; 2010; 2012; 2013). For example the biennial analysis of reviews for 2005–2007 pointed out that 'almost half of

189 children were under one year of age and a third were very young babies under 3 months' (Brandon *et al.*, 2009, p. 20).

In the Brandon *et al.* (2010) report of reviews conducted between 2007–2009, two-thirds of the cases concerned children under five years of age and nearly half of all SCR cases were in relation to babies under one year of age. However in the Brandon *et al.* (2012) report of reviews for 2009–2011, SCRs concerning a baby under one year of age had dropped to just over a third (36%) – a decline of more than 10% from the pattern of earlier years. The authors state that this:

> difference may reflect a change in local decision-making about when to undertake a SCR for non-fatal cases, but might also be attributable to the success in spreading aware- ness among practitioners and community groups of the vul- nerability of babies and the risks of harm they face (Brandon *et al.*, 2012, p. 3).

What the biennial review documents also draw attention to is 'the importance of effective universal services provision for young children' (Brandon *et al.*, 2010, p. i). This is because the major- ity of very young children never come to the attention of chil- dren's social care services, so the role of health visitors, midwives and GPs is really important in identifying this highly vulnerable group. These authors note:

> In the reviews from 2009–11 only 42% of children were get- ting services from children's social care at the time of the child's death or the incident which prompted the review, but also that a significant minority of 21% of children had never been known to this agency. The remaining 37% of cases were either closed or had not been accepted at the point of referral. This reinforces the importance of staff in univer- sal services sharing responsibility for protecting children (Brandon *et al.*, 2012, pp. 136–7).

The most recent biennial review also reports that 'neglect is a background factor in the majority of serious case reviews (60%), and for children of all ages not just the younger children' (Brandon *et al.*, 2012, p. 2; 2013). Daniel (2015, p. 82) argues that existing evidence around the impact of neglect is not being used to best effect and that current protective systems 'are still struggling to provide an effective response to neglected children'. These findings again point to the importance of health visitors providing a universal service to identify and work with vulnerable children across all levels of need. In visiting children and families in their own homes, health visitors have an unparalleled opportunity to identify indicators of neglect.

Policy Directives

Following a considerable, twenty-year period of disinvestment in health visiting, since 2011 policy directives across the UK have reinforced that health visitors have an important role in relation to child protection (DH, 2011; NHS England, 2014). After the tragic death of Baby Peter Connelly in Haringey, London in 2007 and the review of child protection arrangements in England that followed, there has been a greater focus on the health visitor's role in protecting children. Lord Laming's (2009) progress report was very clear in outlining health visitors' responsibilities:

> Health visitors play a key role in child protection, particularly for very young children who are unable to raise the alarm when suffering from abuse or neglect ... the role of health visitors as a universal service seeing all children in their home environment with the potential to develop strong relationships with families is crucially important. A robust health visiting service delivered by highly trained skilled professionals who are alert to potentially vulnerable children can save lives (Laming, 2009, p. 57).

Importantly in 2010 cuts in the health visiting workforce were highlighted in *Giving Children a Healthy Start* (Audit Commission, 2010). This review reported that health visitor numbers had declined in England by 13%, between 2004 and 2008. Later that year, in June 2010, Professor Eileen Munro was appointed by the Coalition government to conduct an independent review of child protection, in recognition that the system of child protection was not working as well as it should (Gove, 2010). Alongside the Munro review, the government announced its commitment to expand the

English health visiting service by increasing the number of health visitors by around 50% (with 4,200 additional health visitors to be in post by 2015) in recognition of how depleted the service had become.

When the final Munro (2011) report was published there was again an emphasis on early identification and the provision of help and support to families as being vitally important in promoting children's well-being. Furthermore several of the report's recommendations were highly relevant to health visitors: for example, the importance of preventative work which 'can do more to reduce abuse and neglect than reactive services', and the importance of early help for children and families (Munro, 2011, p. 7).

What also followed very quickly was a new government vision for health visiting, developed in England through a series of national discussion groups. Also in 2011 a *Health Visitor Implementation Plan: A Call to Action* was published by the Department of Health which illustrated a new service model for health visiting and different service levels. The *Health Visitor Implementation Plan* had three aims:

- to grow the workforce;
- to mobilise the profession;
- to align delivery systems with the changing NHS structures and new local government responsibilities for commissioning children's services (DH, 2011).

The new service model emphasised proportionate universalism, whereby every family is offered a service, which is distributed according to need (Cowley *et al.*, 2012).

The four levels of health visiting service provision are:

- *community* – which is about empowering families with preschool children to build and use community capacity to improve health/welfare outcomes;
- *universal* – for all families with preschool children delivered through the HCP (DH, 2009);
- *universal plus* – a specific care package, including expert information, support and interventions for some families, according to need;
- *universal partnership plus* – intensive and ongoing support for vulnerable families with complex needs;

Throughout all levels, safeguarding and child protection may take place, including high-intensity health visiting work with families as part of multi-agency provision.

Since 2013 England has witnessed an unprecedented investment in health visiting, with professional and service transformation and enhanced training for staff supported through the combined efforts of the Department of Health and Public Health England (DH, 2013b; 2014a). These policy directives have significantly raised the profile of health visiting (DH, 2011; NHS England, 2014). Public Heath England has identified 'ensuring every child has the best start in life' as one of its seven priority areas in its population-based model *From Evidence Into Action: Opportunities to Protect and Improve the Nation's Health* (PHE, 2014).

In England the health visiting service vision has been transformed into a 4–5–6 model of health visiting, which illustrates the five mandated elements of the service (mandated for eighteen months) and six high impact areas (DH, 2015). See Figure 3.1.

To support the transition of commissioning to local authorities and to help inform local decision-making around the commissioning of health visiting and integrated children's early years services, six high impact area documents have been developed, which outline

Figure 3.1 The transformed health visiting service model.

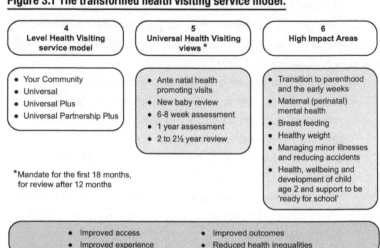

4 Level Health Visiting service model	5 Universal Health Visiting views *	6 High Impact Areas
• Your Community • Universal • Universal Plus • Universal Partnership Plus	• Ante natal health promoting visits • New baby review • 6-8 week assessment • 1 year assessment • 2 to 2½ year review	• Transition to parenthood and the early weeks • Maternal (perinatal) mental health • Breast feeding • Healthy weight • Managing minor illnesses and reducing accidents • Health, wellbeing and development of child age 2 and support to be 'ready for school'

*Mandate for the first 18 months, for review after 12 months

• Improved access
• Improved experience
• Improved outcomes
• Reduced health inequalities

Source: DH (2014a) page 2.

the specific contribution and impact that health visiting can make to improve outcomes for children, families and communities (DH, 2014b). An additional feature of the current policy agenda is the focus on the life course and the negative impact that child abuse and neglect and other childhood adversity may have on long-term physical and mental health, education and social outcomes (APPG, 2015).

Health visiting's distinctive contribution[2] to child protection

The *2015–2016 National Health Visiting Core Service Specification* clearly highlights the health visiting role in child protection and safeguarding children as 'essential components of the service' (NHS England, 2014, p. 15). If the service is properly resourced health visitors can make a unique contribution to safeguarding and protecting children. Examples are given below of safeguarding activity within the different levels of the English service model. Obviously this will reflect a range of family-based interventions, which will depend on an infant, child and family's individual needs.

Community level

This might involve early identification of risk factors – for example through an examination of epidemiological data, population demographics or benchmarking local data from the Child and Maternal (CHiMat) Health Intelligence Network's Children and Young People's Health Outcomes Framework – to address local health concerns. It may include trying to influence policies affecting community needs such as around safe play areas and school initiatives to keep children safe online.

Universal level

Health visitors are ideally placed to advise about normal child development patterns and to provide parenting support. As leaders of the HCP (DH, 2009a) for families with preschool children, health visitors have many opportunities to use their skills to assess children's and their parent's health needs, and work with colleagues in the health visiting team to provide preventative packages of care (DH, 2009a; 2011). For example, a mother or father might seek guidance or reassurance from a health visitor, which would constitute the beginning of early intervention, preventative work. This might lead to a health visitor suggesting ways of understanding a baby's emotional needs, perhaps supporting a change in parenting pattern through the provision of evidence-based advice or in some cases referring for specialist assessment and support. The importance of such early intervention work with new parents is extremely important in promoting children's well-being and in identifying risk factors early (Field, 2010; Allen, 2011a; Munro, 2011; WAVE Trust, 2013). Individual work with a child and family would take place only once a health or development need has been identified and this individual focus is not reached unless the whole population has access to a universal HCP (DH, 2009a).

Universal plus level
Following a HCP (DH, 2009a) health and development review a health visitor may identify – or a parent may express – health needs that require short-term targeted intervention or support. An illustration of this could be around the management of an infant's sleep problem. In some situations where health needs are identified, the health visitor may enable parents to join local peer groups to support their parenting requirements. Without a universal service, those families highlighted in the Health Visitor Implementation Plan (DH, 2011, p. 10) as requiring additional services 'some of the time' or 'vulnerable families requiring ongoing additional support' are unlikely to be identified and helped.

Universal partnership plus level
Health visitors must have the skills to identify families with high levels of risk factors and lower levels of protective factors (DH, 2009a). This may include extremely vulnerable families where multiple adverse issues are present, such as severe financial difficulties, domestic violence or 'the toxic trio' of parental mental illness, problem drug and alcohol use and domestic violence. Health visiting at this level may include working with parents with complex difficulties to build their coping and resilience skills and support protective factors including self-efficacy. A Common Assessment Framework may be completed and evidence-based intensive

programmes offered through children centres to develop parenting skills, access to support groups or community resources to reduce isolation or referral to specialists. It is generally recognised that establishing positive working relationships with vulnerable families does require considerable skill, time and determination. The use of highly developed and sensitive listening and observation skills are key (Cowley *et al.*, 2013). Where targeted work does not result in an improved situation or where a family consistently avoids or is unable to achieve an improved situation for a child, there will be a need to discuss the child's situation with children's social care (Appleton and Clemerson-Trew, 2008).

Safeguarding and child protection
Some children will need to be referred to children's social care. As the WHO notes:

> Maltreatment and other adversity in childhood may cause toxic levels of stress, which impair brain development and may lead to the adoption of health-harming behaviour, poorer mental and physical health, worse educational and social outcomes throughout the life-course and intergenerational transmission of violence (WHO, United Nations Office on Drugs and Crime and United Nations Development Programme, 2014).

If a health visitor considers that a:

> child may be a child in need as defined in the Children Act 1989, or that the child has suffered significant harm or is likely to do so, a referral should be made immediately to local authority children's social care (HM Government, 2015, p. 14).

Health visitors should be fully conversant with their LSCB child protection procedures and the clinical guideline *When to Suspect Child Maltreatment* (National Collaborating Centre for Women's and Children's Health, 2009). The latter provides practical and helpful guidance around the alerting features of child maltreatment and when to 'consider', or when to 'suspect', child abuse and neglect.

Where an initial child protection conference (CPC) is called and there are preschool children in the family, health visitors will be part of the multi-agency, decision-making process in considering if a child is at continuing risk of significant harm and whether a formal child protection plan is implemented. Health visitors should also be active members of repeat CPCs and core groupwork. It will be usual for a health visitor to have ongoing contact with a child and family, in the clinic and home environments, where there are formal child protection procedures in place to deliver preventative health interventions. Health visitors will be part of the multi-agency support package working to improve the child and family health outcomes, predicting, identifying and assessing where extra support is needed and building resilience and protective factors. This aspect of the role has received little research attention (so is rather invisible outside the professional network) and is a challenging aspect of the work requiring high-level professional skills and authoritative practice (Sidebotham, 2013).

Conclusion

The vision set out in the English Health Visitor Implementation Plan was about:

> …making sure the appropriate health visiting services form part of the high intensity multi-agency services for families where there are safeguarding and child protection concerns (DH, 2011, p. 10).

Despite the national roll out of the Health Visitor Implementation Plan, realistically it will take a number of years to rebuild the expertise of the health visiting workforce which was so depleted over twenty years. It takes time, nurturing and experience to build new health visitor's skills and expertise, upskill the existing workforce and improve staff confidence and morale. However the profession has received considerable support to do this and is now firmly on the policy agenda. Furthermore, because of its unique home visiting element, health visiting continues to have a distinctive contribution to make to safeguarding and protecting children. This chapter has presented the case that, if health visiting services are properly resourced, these professionals are ideally placed through the *Healthy Child Programme* (DH, 2009a) to identify children who with their families require expert advice, support and guidance, including those children who are potentially vulnerable and at risk of abuse and neglect.

Summary

Health visitors' focus is on population health and this chapter has examined the contribution of health visiting to safeguarding children and child protection practice. It has emphasised the distinctive contribution of health visitors' work in child protection practice, acknowledging that this should be part of a continuum of public health activity including universal preventative work and identifying and working with vulnerable children and their families, as well as protecting children from abuse and neglect. A key feature of the health visitors' role is that these public health professionals make home visits to all children and their families; they are thus in a unique position to provide a targeted service according to need, to work with vulnerable families to build resilience and to identify children at risk of abuse and neglect.

Notes
1 This chapter has been adapted with kind permission of the publishers from a paper first published in *Community Practitioner*.
2. The distinctive contribution of the Principles of Health Visiting has been outlined by the CHPVA (2007).

CHAPTER 4

Looking beyond the UK

Caroline Bradbury-Jones, University of Birmingham
Eija Paavailainen, University of Tampere
Julie Taylor, University of Birmingham

Introduction

The previous chapters have explored the issue of child maltreatment in relation to public health nursing and have focused primarily on the contribution of SCPHN in Britain to child protection practice. In this chapter the scope is broadened and a pan-European perspective taken. A scoping of current practices from a number of countries in Europe is presented. Variations and similarities are highlighted and Finland is used as a more focused example of how this area of public health nursing practice is developing. The structure of strengths, weaknesses, opportunities and threats [SWOT] is used to analyse and critique the role of public health nurses in relation to child protection across Europe. Increasing mobility of the nursing workforce across Europe makes this a timely and useful analysis and one that sheds light on the current status and future opportunities for public health nurses' child protection roles across different countries.

Background

Globalisation is a phenomenon that has attracted considerable interest over the past few decades among researchers, policymakers, sociologists and epidemiologists. It is marked by increased ease in communication and movement of goods and people across the world. Expressed quite simply – the world has become a smaller place (Bradbury-Jones, 2009). Regarding Europe, under the Schengen Agreement 1985, signatory states have abolished all internal borders in lieu of a single external border. This has been incorporated into the EU legal framework by the Treaty of Amsterdam 1997 and has provided an EU territory within which free movement of people is guaranteed (europa.eu, 2014). The implication is unprecedented mobility of the population across Europe.

Where there are people, there are accompanying health and social issues. Where there is globalisation, movement of populations and shifting demographics, there need to be appropriate health and social care interventions and responses. With this in mind it is no longer sufficient for nurses to look inwards to their own countries and contexts in order to understand issues of relevance and importance. Instead an outward perspective is necessary – one in which they look to other countries, learn from them and share the insights gained from the broader perspective. Fortunately it is now easier than ever for nurses to exchange experiences and to learn from one another. This chapter is one such example. The authors are three nurse researchers in Europe with interests in public health approaches to understanding child maltreatment. Globalisation has allowed the authors to communicate readily with each other and with other nurse researchers across Europe to investigate the role of public health nurses in different countries, particularly regarding child protection. Globalisation is recognised as having made an impact on the social, economic and political contexts in which child maltreatment occurs (Gilbert *et al.*, 2011). So this chapter draws together the individual issues of public health nursing and child protection, and examines them in the context of a globalised world.

Over the past years there has been mounting interest in making comparisons of child protection systems across countries (Freymond and Cameron, 2006; Gilbert *et al.*, 2011; Munro and Manful, 2012). Gilbert *et al.*'s (2011) analysis was across ten countries: England, Norway, Finland, Denmark, Germany, Belgium, Netherlands, Sweden, USA and Canada. Unsurprisingly Gilbert *et al.* observed differences in child protection systems across countries. They categorised these according to the extent to which their systems were characterised by either 'child protection' or 'family service' orientation. Gilbert *et al.* (2011) describe a distinction that in child protection oriented systems abuse is conceived as requiring protection of children from perpetrators, whereas family service orientation is considered to be a family problem that responds to help and support. They suggest that in the 1990s Anglo-American countries tended to be oriented towards child protection, while Continental European and Nordic countries approached the problem of child maltreatment from a family service orientation (Gilbert *et al.,.* 2011). Their analysis identifies shifting patterns that will be discussed later in the chapter.

Latterly Munro and Manful (2012) have compared systems in England and Norway (including also Australia and USA). They too found differences in terms of how child maltreatment is defined, classified and addressed. These previous analyses have illuminated differences in safeguarding systems generally. But the focus here is concerned specifically with the role of public health nurses within these systems. We are interested in this because there is currently scant understanding of the similarities and differences of public health nurses' safeguarding role across Europe. Yet this level of understanding is crucial. Summarising the nuanced differences in their scope and practice is important in gauging the extent to which different countries recognise the important role that public health nurses play in the support and surveillance of children (Ministry of Social Affairs and Health, 2013; Scottish Government, 2014a). Such comparisons also allow for policy and practice in one country to be benchmarked against others (Munro and Manful, 2012).

In this chapter some of the key issues are highlighted that can be learned from taking an outward-looking, pan-European perspective. The primary focus is to present work that the authors have undertaken to appraise current public health nursing practices in Europe. Findings from an expert panel drawn from ten European countries are presented and the similarities in terms of scope of practice and safeguarding practices are critiqued. One of the authors (Eija Paavilainen) draws on her insider perspectives of public health nursing in Finland to present a case example and use this to make comparisons with child protection practices in the other countries.

It is known from the authors' own public health practice and research that there is considerable variability across roles of public health nurses (and their equivalents) in Europe. Differences exist in provision of services: in some countries all families of young children are allocated to a public health nurse at birth; in others the role of

public health nurse does not even exist; and in many further countries a role exists somewhere between these extremes. Additionally
and somewhat confusingly there are also variations in terminology –
even within countries. For example, as discussed in other parts of this
book, in the UK the terms 'specialist community public health nurse
(SCPHN)', 'public health nurse' and 'health visitor' tend to be used
synonymously. They are however distinct, as health visiting is part
of public health nursing (along with school nursing). Public health
nursing is thus a much broader term and for consistency it is one that
is used throughout this chapter.

Public Health Nursing across Europe: A Rapid Appraisal

In early 2013, as preparatory work for this chapter, we used the networks of nurses in Europe to collate information about child protection systems and practices in different countries. Specifically we
were interested in how these were related to the role of public health
nurses. Nurses from ten European countries were contacted via
email and were invited to respond to the following questions:

- Do you have public health nurses in your country?
- Do public health nurses have a specific role in promoting the
  health and welfare of children (as opposed to other groups such
  as older people)?
- Do public health nurses have a specific role in child protection?
- If yes to 2 and 3, what is their role? For example, if they were
  concerned that a child was being abused:
  (a) What would they do?
  (b) What would their involvement be?
  (c) What systems are in place to protect that child?

We want to be clear that the intention here is not to masquer-
ade this as an empirical study; it was not. It was a rapid appraisal
using our extensive collective networks of public health nurses across
Europe. The aim was to gain insight into practices, procedures and
child protection remit. Despite the rather unsophisticated approach
to the appraisal, it did provide useful insights. Responses to questions
1–3 are presented in Table 4.1. Of the ten nurses, eight reported that
they had public health nurses in their countries and of these all had
either a partial or specific role in promoting the health and welfare of

Table 4.1 Responses to rapid appraisal exercise.

Country	Q.1 Do you have public health nurses in your country?	Q.2 Do public health nurses have a specific role in promoting the health and welfare of children (as opposed to other groups such as older people)?	Q.3 Do public health nurses have a specific role in child protection?
Cyprus	yes	partial	no
Denmark	yes	yes	yes
Finland	yes	yes	yes
Germany	no	no	no
Norway	yes	yes	yes
Portugal	yes	partial	partial
Republic of Ireland	yes	yes	yes
Sweden	yes	yes	yes
Switzerland	no	no	no
United Kingdom	yes	yes	yes

children. The majority of nurses reported that public health nurses in their country had a specific role in child protection. Given the scope of this chapter, this was the issue to which we gave most attention and we were particularly interested in responses to question four. The qualitative descriptions that follow begin to illustrate similarities and differences across the small sample. We were able to discern differences in public health nurses' child protection roles:

'This role is not necessarily played by public health nurses (Portugal).'

'The public health nurses do have a responsibility in identifying child abuse. The health nurses' role is to prevent, and some of their duty is to give guidance to parents, individual or in groups. They have a special responsibility to identify vulnerable families and parents (Norway).'

'While in principle caring for vulnerable children is within the role for nurses in general, the term 'child protection' is not in frequent use nor is it used to refer to a particular remit (Cyprus).'

We were interested in the initial responses of public health nurses when faced with suspected child maltreatment. In terms of the similarities, the statutory responsibility to report such cases was captured across a number of countries:

'An initial referral is made to the social work department and participation at CPCs or providing evidence in court proceedings and maybe involved in the operationalisation of supervision orders (Republic of Ireland).'

'All nurses (and teachers and other categories) who worked with children were required by law to report to the social authority any suspicion of child abuse (Sweden).'

'Public health nurses in the UK had a duty to report suspected child abuse or neglect and they did this in the first instance to social services. Depending on the severity and perceived imminent danger to a child, they could also call the police, but this was quite unusual (UK).'

'If a nurse (specialist or not) in her/his work suspected abuse or negligence (and the same applied for a teacher, and even a citizen), they had to notify the local 'protection committee of children and young people'. This committee evaluated the situation and articulated the adequate responses (in terms of family court, health, education, social work) and so on (Portugal).'

'If the public nurses were concerned about a child being abused, they gave notice to the child protection services (established in every municipality) as required by law. There was special legislation concerning child protection and if health professionals and social care workers were concerned, they had to contact the child protection services (Norway).'

In addition to the initial actions, we wanted to glean insights into the nature of ongoing public health nurse involvement with families where there were child protection concerns and the nature of child protection services and systems. Again there were more similarities than differences across the sample, with public health nurses playing a central role:

'Public health nurses often worked within networks collaborating with parents, teachers, staff in kindergartens, doctors, midwives etc. When there was a special problem, relevant professionals got together, analysed problems and initiated interventions. Public health nurses were often co-ordinators of such work groups (Norway).'

'The public health nurse might be involved in further actions i.e. supporting the family, checking up etc. The family doctor/GP might get involved too. Depending on the problem, the nurse would co-operate with relevant parties (Denmark).'

'There were 'protection committees of children and young people'. These committees were multi-professional... and they evaluated and followed the cases of children at risk (Portugal).'

There were however some differences across countries, with some having limited scope for public health nurses in a child protection capacity: for example, Germany, Switzerland and Cyprus.

So far in the chapter we have begun to identify some of the patterns of practice across the countries included in the rapid appraisal. Using a case example from Finland (see below), we can now explore these further.

Public health nursing and child protection in Finland: A case example

Public health nurses in Finland have been specially educated to assess families' and children's physical and psychosocial health and well-being and any threats to these. They are thus in a key position to identify and intervene in children and families' problems, in particular regarding child maltreatment. This reflects the picture created in the rapid appraisal, where respondents in eight countries (including Finland) reported that public health nurses in their countries had either a partial or specific role in promoting the health and welfare of children, with the majority having a specific role in child protection.

Although most children in Finland were healthy and well-nurtured, like their counterparts in other countries, some children experienced disadvantage and adversity. Increasingly many families faced multiple challenges, with increasing numbers of children known to child protection services. Correspondingly greater numbers of children and adolescents were accessing more mental health services (Ministry of Social Affairs and Health, 2013). Research in Finland (Lepistö *et al.,* 2011) shows that children and young people experienced a wide range of maltreatment at home, including physical, emotional and sexual violence, neglect and witnessing of violence between parents. The same forms of child maltreatment were observed in other countries in Europe and beyond (Gilbert *et al.,* 2009b).

For developing working practices concerning child maltreatment identification in Finland, national guidelines had been published by the Nursing
Research Foundation (www.hotus.fi/; Paavilainen and Flinck, 2013). They
were based on a systematic review of multidisciplinary literature show-
ing that child maltreatment had attracted considerable research interest.
Based on earlier research evidence, the guidelines presented the risk factors, signs and symptoms and principles for identifying and intervening in
suspected child maltreatment. Risk factors were presented concerning:
the child (for example age, crying, exhibiting challenging behaviour); parents (for example young age, substance misuse, mental health problems);
and the family (for example family violence, many children in the family).
By understanding these risks and also signs of maltreatment (including
physical signs or symptoms in the child's behaviour), it was possible for
public health nurses to consider them in their involvement with families and
children. By identifying possible risks, it was possible to assess a family's
situation and find ways to offer appropriate support. Such support might
include offering advice regarding child development, how to manage difficult behaviour and exploring couple relationships. Typically this would be
in the context of home visits. It might also involve a referral to child protection services; after this, social workers were responsible for assessing
the situation, with the involvement of other professionals. The legislation
in Finland, as in other Nordic countries, had been developed early when
compared to many other European countries.

The guidelines placed considerable emphasis on multi-professional
team work and how models of multi-professional practices could be
developed across many organisations and municipalities. The guidelines
are in the process of being updated (Paavilainen and Flinck, 2014). In the
UK there have been similar recent updates in England and Wales (HM
Government, 2015) and the title of the national guidance there emphasises this multi-professional approach: *Working Together to Safeguard
Children*.

Conclusion of the Finnish case example

Overall, as a case example, Finland represents a fairly typical picture
of public health nursing and child protection in comparison with
most other countries included in our review. While there is some
infrastructure, policy and culture to protect children, things are far
from perfect and there remains much to be done. Legislation and
research based guidelines concerning child maltreatment encourage
the development of advanced practices in working with families and
children. There are also good public health nursing traditions, which
are being developed to shift emphasis from physical health issues
towards increasing focus on socio-emotional health of children and

families. Additionally systematic development of research based practices in working with children and families aim to detect families' needs for support as early as possible and find ways of supporting families according to their needs.

Based on national evaluations, statistics pertaining to non-accidental injury and individual cases of child deaths in Finland (Ministry of Justice, 2014), an increased emphasis upon developing and updating practices on knowledge exchange and multi-professional work is evident. This may be indicative of the shift in focus mentioned earlier, which retains a family service orientation yet incorporates a system that is focused on child protection.

Reflections on the rapid appraisal and Finnish case study

Gilbert *et al.* (2011) observe that current approaches to protecting children are far more complex than a few decades ago and there has been a shift in patterns from the dichotomised approaches of the 1990s. For example in England there is clear evidence of refocusing practice in a way that family support is maximised, and in countries that had previously operated to a family service model there is now more concern about harm to children. They suggest that this is well illustrated in all the Nordic countries, including the case study country, Finland. Although we did not look for the same approaches as Gilbert, and colleagues, our appraisal has been useful in highlighting differences in systems across Europe.

Despite its value however there are some limitations to the appraisal that need to be acknowledged. Firstly, we were hampered by lack of consistency across the countries regarding understandings and terminology in relation to public health nursing: for example:

- The term [public health nurse] exists, but the role is rather ambiguous. It represents a combination of district, community and school nurses (Cyprus).
- They are called health nurses (Norway).
- Public health nurses are health visitors and school nurses. It is a broad term (UK).

Secondly, like Munro and Manful (2012), we also grappled with lack of consistency regarding definitions of abuse and neglect. So with reference to Finland as the case study country, although child maltreatment clearly exists as a problem, it is interesting to note that the actual terms 'child abuse' and 'child neglect' barely exist. According to Gilbert *et al.* (2011) this reflects Finland's historical approach to child welfare thinking (although this may change along with shifts in focus already discussed). It also serves to illustrate how the concepts and problems may be similar, but there are complexities in making meaningful comparisons across countries. Lastly, although we drew on the expertise of a pool of nurse scientists across Europe, this was a limited and self-selecting sample and was not necessarily representative of the sector. Nonetheless the chapter so far has formed the platform for the final discussions within the chapter.

Public health nursing and child protection in Europe: A SWOT analysis

Manzano-García and Ayala-Calvo (2014) have undertaken a SWOT analysis of nursing across Europe, and inspiration has been drawn from this in the structure of this final discussion section. Here, we use the structure of SWOT to analyse and critique the role of public health nurses in relation to child protection across Europe.

Strengths

Unlike Manzano-García and Ayala-Calvo (2014), who state that the identity of nursing is weak, we conclude that the identity of public health nursing is strong. Most countries have public health nurses and most of these have an explicit child protection role. The recent Children and Young People Bill in Scotland (Scottish Government, 2014b) places health visitors at the heart of surveillance for children under age five, and there is renewed commitment and funding from all parties across the UK to increase the numbers of health visitors over the next few years. Across Europe as a whole there is a sustained move towards early childhood interventions that work not just with the child but also with the family and the environment (European Agency for Development in Special Needs Education, 2005). A current, nine-country study is responding to the European Competence Initiative (ECI) on early childhood intervention, providing training to empower health professionals, teachers and social workers to support parents (ECI, 2014).

Manzano-García and Ayala-Calvo (2014) suggest that public health nurses have greater independence than other nurses and in the context of child protection this may place them in a better position to adapt their work to those children and families in greatest need. We suggest therefore that the independence, universality and focus on the early years in public health nursing are a significant strength for child protection.

Weaknesses
However there are weaknesses as well. Some public health nurses across Europe see child protection work as other peoples' business, as not central to their own role but something for teachers or police or social workers. This is not helped by variation in legislation across countries, and there are some cultural differences regarding what constitutes child abuse: for example, in Finland corporal punishment is against the law and physical punishment of children is seen as maltreatment. In some countries physical punishment is still quite acceptable and the smacking debate continues (Zolotor and Puzia, 2010).

There is often a lack of knowledge sharing across professions, with each working independently of each other (Ofsted, 2011). Probably every report on child protection systems or on investigations into the death or severe maltreatment of a child makes comment on the lack of inter-agency working and sharing of knowledge (Sidebotham, 2012). It seems this is played out across Europe, with some countries being further along a trajectory of multi-agency trust, knowledge sharing and working together than others. It appears that we still have some way to go.

Opportunities
But when we examine the child protection role of public health nurses in Europe there are opportunities. Globalisation has made it easier than ever to share knowledge and it is not unusual to be involved in discussion with colleagues from a range of countries. New and emerging technologies make this even easier. Funding streams such as Horizon 2020 (see http://ec.europa.eu/programmes/horizon2020/en/) provide opportunities for generating shared research

knowledge and using research to move forward. The case study from Finland demonstrates the utility of finding out what is happening in other European countries and exploring their relevance to our own contexts and countries. Cultural adaptation may not be as difficult as expected. There are actually more similarities than differences across Europe, providing a great chance to work together in progressing the child protection agenda.

Threats

Any SWOT analysis ends with the threats to the subject and there are indeed some inherent ones to the child protection role of public health nurses in Europe. The emotional labour associated with child protection work is high and is exacerbated by cutbacks in services (Appleton, 2012). Decision-making can be fraught with anxiety, and the current economic environment means that many child protection services or those that support them have been cut. In such cases thresholds for child protection rise, a more or less clear route to tragedy. It is estimated that for every eight children in need of protection only one comes to the attention of the child protection system (Jütte *et al.*, 2014). As such, Jütte and colleagues suggest that the child protection system should be viewed comparably with emergency services in health, treating the most serious and damaging cases. Public health nurses with high caseloads may put further pressure on to that 'emergency service'.

As in general nursing, migration of the workforce across Europe means that the nursing workforce in some countries, particularly those in the east of Europe is depleted. Such widespread mobility means greater opportunities for trafficking and the increase in refugees from countries in war and conflict exacerbates this threat. Children who have spent much of their lives in terror from war or displacement from conflict have particular care needs. For example evidence from a number of European countries including Sweden, Denmark, the Netherlands and UK shows that children within displaced families are likely to experience socio-economic disadvantage and poor mental health, especially post-traumatic stress disorder (Fazel *et al.*, 2012). Public health nurses play an important role in supporting such families. It may be however that the problem is happening more extensively and with greater rapidity than we are able to muster the required responses.

Conclusion

In this chapter we have explored the nature of public health nursing and child protection at a European-wide level. It appears that there are more similarities than differences. An important issue that we have identified is inconsistency in terminology and meanings around the role itself (such as health visiting, public health nursing, health nursing) and the specific focus (child protection, safeguarding, preventing child maltreatment etc.). Linguistic and cultural interpretations make an analysis across countries difficult. However despite these challenges we hope that the rapid appraisal, case example and SWOT analysis presented in this chapter have offered some useful insights beyond those previously available.

Summary

The rapid appraisal presented in the chapter provided a glimpse into child protection systems and practices and their relationship to public health nursing from a number of European countries. We have highlighted the similarities that exist across some countries such as Scandinavia and UK. But we have also shown that other countries have limited scope for public health nurses in a child protection capacity. Of course, it could be that other nurses are assuming this role or supporting public health nurses in this capacity. We have used the case example of Finland to reflect on the rapid appraisal and to draw on existing policies and research. We hope that this has illuminated further some of the issues raised. Combined with the SWOT analysis, we have captured the status quo, and there are also opportunities for the future. What would be useful now is a fuller description of public health nursing and child protection across Europe to be researched and for this to be robustly and empirically grounded.

CHAPTER 5

Safeguarding and child protection: The important contribution of the wider nursing and midwifery workforce

Catherine Powell, Safeguarding Children Consultant, UK

Introduction

Chapter 5 outlines the contribution of the wider nursing and midwifery workforce in ensuring the safety and well-being of children and young people. The first part of the chapter highlights the practice, policy and professional guidance that provide the mandate for a whole profession responsibility to embed a proactive and responsive approach to the prevention of child maltreatment and the recognition and referral of child protection concerns. The second part considers some examples from practice which reflect healthcare journeys that may be experienced by children, young people and their families, and the opportunities that these present for meaningful intervention to protect children from harm.

This chapter considers the contribution of the wider nursing and midwifery workforce (by which is meant registered nurses and midwives who are delivering care in a range of healthcare settings) to a public health approach to safeguarding and child protection. The practice, policy and professional guidance that support this approach are outlined and case examples from a range of practice settings are discussed. The case examples illustrate the potential for nurses and midwives to embrace the principles of public health (at primary, secondary and tertiary levels of prevention) and deliver responsive and supportive care that can help to safeguard and promote the welfare of children and young people. Of key consideration here is the healthcare 'journey' (see Munro, 2011) taken by children and young people and their parents or carers. This reflects the potential for family members to have contact with, and care delivery from, nurses and midwives working in a variety of hospital and community settings. In turn this contact can provide unrivalled opportunities to ensure the well-being of children in the family, even where the primary client is the parent.

Practice, policy and professional guidance

The remit for an all-profession responsibility for safeguarding and child protection is well-embedded in policy documents and professional guidance; examples of these are highlighted later in this section. A helpful starting point, especially for nurses and midwives who may have concerns about their role in this potentially challenging area of practice, is to consider how well the core attributes of their profession dovetail with those of safeguarding and child protection work.

Powell (2007) discusses the findings from the extensive consultation undertaken by the Royal College of Nursing (RCN) in the UK that sought to define the role of the 'nurse' in contemporary society and health systems and draws parallels between the key concepts that underpin practice in both arenas. (Midwifery and health visiting are inclusive in the RCN use of the term 'nurse'.) The aim of the RCN's enquiry was to move away from a stereotypical and gendered view (often held by those outside the profession) of nurses as subservient handmaidens caring for the institutional sick to one that comprises not only caring (which is central) but also the attributes of promoting health, prevention, minimising suffering, empowerment, partnership and holism (RCN, 2003). Partnership, the RCN note, is with patients (clients, service users), their families and the wider multidisciplinary team. As Powell (2007) argues, these are also core attributes of safeguarding and child protection work, and they could be usefully exercised in protecting children and young people and in demonstrating the scope and value of nursing and midwifery practice to commissioners as well as to multidisciplinary and multi-agency partners.

The care delivered by the contemporary nursing and midwifery practitioner, which takes account of promoting health and wellbeing and of working in partnership with individuals, families and other professionals reflects requirements for safeguarding children's roles and responsibilities within the wider child protection system. This work includes the early identification of additional needs and provision of parental support, as well as the recognition and referral of children and young people who are at risk of or suffering from child abuse and neglect. It is quite possible that nurses and midwives are making a meaningful contribution to safeguarding children without this being made explicit. For example if safeguarding (as defined in statutory guidance for England) includes ensuring that children are provided with 'safe and effective care' (HM Government, 2015, p. 5) then any action taken by a nurse or midwife to promote developmentally appropriate, nurturing and responsive care by parents is de facto safeguarding practice. If parents or carers are experiencing chronic physical or mental health problems, are learning-disabled or substance misusers, then the nursing or midwifery interventions may be particularly crucial in ensuring the best outcomes for the child.

The theme of wider responsibilities for safeguarding and promoting the welfare of children is reflected by Jütte *et al.* (2014), who emphasise the importance of this being a 'whole systems' approach, involving all those who work with children, young people and their families, rather than being the sole responsibility of any one agency such as children's social care. The size and scale of the professional workforce is an important consideration here. While the increase in the numbers of health visitors in line with recent policy (DH, 2011) is to be welcomed, health visitors remain a small proportion of the national nursing workforce in the UK. In practice children, young people and their parents and carers will be in receipt of much of their healthcare provision from the wider family of nursing. For some families this contact with the wider nursing workforce may be particularly extensive. For example, if the widely acknowledged risks for child maltreatment – pre-term birth, childhood physical or learning disability, chronic disease and/or parental difficulties such as mental health, learning disability or substance misuse problems, etc. – are added in, the pattern of engagement with a broad range of health services (and thus nursing and midwifery professionals) becomes clear.

'Everyone's Responsibility'

The safeguarding and child protection remit of the nursing workforce is embedded in policy and legislation. According to the statutory guidance, safeguarding children is 'everyone's responsibility' (HM Government, 2015, p. 5) and health services, whether commissioned or provided by the NHS or by independent healthcare organisations, have particular duties in this respect. While by no means inclusive, the guidance makes some attempt to 'list' the professionals who will see children, young people and their families in healthcare settings, including nurses, midwives and health visitors. The guidance is important because it sets out the expectations of agencies in responding to concerns about the well-being of children and how different players in the child protection system need to work together to ensure effective collaboration. Importantly the provisions of the guidance will be reflected in the expectations of LSCB and individual organisational (health services) policies and procedures.

While the statutory guidance is aimed at all those working in the various agencies and organisations that come into contact with children, young people and their families, more detail of the knowledge, skills and competence required by nurses and midwives (and other health professionals) to ensure effective safeguarding and child protection practice are provided in the Royal College of Paediatrics and Child Health's (RCPCH) 'intercollegiate document' (RCPCH, 2014). This guidance, now in its third edition, has been signed up by all the key health professional bodies including the RCN, Royal College of Midwives (RCM) and Community Practitioners' and Health Visitors' Association (CPHVA).

The intercollegiate document tailors requirements to specific roles within healthcare delivery, with the expectations of achieving a particular 'level' of knowledge, skills and competence. Evidence of achievement may be used to underpin professional regulatory activities such as appraisal and revalidation. The document states that nurses and midwives who have 'any' contact with children, young people or their parents or carers require a minimum of 'level two', which includes, among an array of expectations, the requirement to demonstrate 'an understanding of the public health significance of child maltreatment including epidemiology and financial impact' (RCPCH, 2014, p. 15). Level three (which incorporates the previous levels) reflects the learning needs of those who may be required to contribute to assessing, planning, intervening and evaluating the needs of children and young people, including parenting capacity, where there are safeguarding concerns (see Table 5.1).

Table 5.1 Practitioners requiring Level Three safeguarding and child protection training.

- adult mental health practitioners;
- child and adolescent mental health practitioners;
- urgent and unscheduled care practitioners;
- learning disability practitioners;
- substance misuse practitioners;
- sexual health practitioners;
- children's services (paediatrics) practitioners;
- maternity service practitioners;
- health visitors;
- school nurses.

Source: (RCPCH, 2014)

Likewise, the professional regulators – the NMC – have an expectation that pre-registration educational programmes will prepare practitioners to be responsive to child protection issues and to gain an understanding of public health principles, priorities and practice (NMC, 2010). Furthermore, in practising within the provisions of the NMC 'Code of Conduct' (currently under review), all nurses and midwives are expected to make a disclosure if they believe that someone is at risk of harm (NMC, 2008).

Given the underpinning policy and professional remit and responsibility for safeguarding and child protection it is important that nurses and midwives have access to support and clinical supervision, as well as information that will help them in their practice. The National Institute for Health and Clinical Excellence (NICE) guidance on child maltreatment seeks to 'raise awareness and help healthcare professionals who are not specialists in child protection' (National Collaborating Centre for Women's and Children's Health, 2009, p. 4) by alerting them to clinical features that should lead to a consideration or suspicion of child maltreatment, as well as when it may be excluded. Importantly it reminds those from the wider nursing and midwifery family that they are not expected to be diagnosticians in this respect. However as Powell (2011) notes, knowledge of childcare and development together with good assessment skills are essential for safeguarding and child protection work, as this will help in supporting parenting, recognising the possible concerns and referring on to specialists or lead statutory agencies for further assessment where needed. In addition it should be noted here that, because nurses, midwives and health visitors come into contact with a range of children, young people and their families, they are particularly well placed to identify indicators of concern or patterns of behaviour that fall outside of the 'norm' and that this is the case whether they are providing care directly to a child or young person, a parent or a member of the family.

Prevention

The evidence to support strategies that prevent child maltreatment at an individual, societal and political level is also building. This includes the recognition of the importance of the provision of parenting support programmes that help to ensure safe, stable and nurturing environments for children and young people. There is 'compelling evidence' (Davies and Ward, 2012, p. 140) to support the need for early intervention to prevent the likelihood of child maltreatment where there are parental difficulties such as domestic violence and abuse, substance misuse, learning disabilities, mental health problems, housing problems, family breakdown, social exclusion and other key stressors. An example here is the midwife who makes sensitive enquiry as to the possibility of domestic violence or abuse during pregnancy and who supports and signposts the woman to appropriate services.

In addition to the obvious links with care provision within mental health and substance misuse services there is a public health imperative for the wider nursing and midwifery workforce. The evidence of the burden of poor health arising from child maltreatment sets the scene for the professions to move beyond reactive individual care delivery in response to the myriad of health problems caused by for example type-two diabetes or alcohol addiction, to a proactive stance. This approach would seek to understand the possible explanations for these health problems, to address the causes and to embed strategies to prevent future occurrence across populations.

So far this chapter has sought to highlight the recognition of the safeguarding and child protection contribution of nursing and midwifery in practice, policy and professional guidance. It has also considered the scale and impact of child maltreatment on the health and well-being of individuals, families and communities, as well as the imperative for prevention. The final section aims to bring together the themes already raised by considering the child (and parents' or carers') 'journey' through the healthcare system.

The child's healthcare journey

Children and young people in the UK have an entitlement to a programme of universal healthcare provision that aims to ensure their optimum health and well-being from pre-birth to nineteen years of age. In England this public health-oriented approach is known as the HCP (DH, 2009a, 2009b) and is delivered by midwives, health visitors and school nurses with support from other health professionals such as practitioners from primary care services, where the role of the practice nurse is notable (e.g. immunisation clinics). The universal approach, which provides advice and support on parenting as well as monitoring child health and development, has been noted to be effective and acceptable (Barlow and Calam, 2011). The programme also has the flexibility to ensure that children, young people and families with greater needs receive an enhanced service, that is, the 'universal plus' and 'universal partnership plus' provision, which is usually delivered in conjunction with a wider group of health and social care professionals. The tiers of additional support are in line with the concept of 'progressive universalism' introduced as a policy response to high-profile child protection cases, while the model for care delivery has 'safeguarding' as a cross-cutting priority throughout. The difficulty arises however when there is either a mismatch of expectations or else children, young people and families fail to access the programme.

In addition to the universal healthcare provision described above, children, young people and their families are highly likely to access and attend a range of other healthcare services. Most commonly this will be for additional services provided by general practitioners and their staff, but it may also include urgent and unscheduled care provision and secondary paediatric or specialist care. Health professionals in these services should be alert to any safeguarding or child protection concerns, as well as be enabled to provide parental support and advice. Furthermore failure to attend (or not being taken to) an appointment or not allowing access for a home visit is an important safeguarding concern that is known to feature in serious childcare cases (Powell and Appleton, 2012). For sixteen and seventeen year olds the interface at the point of transition to adult services is also significant and may be a point of particular vulnerability (Wolfe *et al.*, 2014).

Parents and carers may also be in receipt of healthcare services to support a chronic physical health need, or a mental health, learning disability or substance misuse problem. These issues are known to be associated with a greater risk of child maltreatment, and the adult practitioner has a responsibility to make an assessment of the impact of these difficulties on the ability of a parent to provide safe and effective care to their child or children and ensure additional support accordingly.

There are a number of 'windows of opportunity' for a midwifery or nursing professional to take action to ensure a child or young person's health and well-being. Three examples of involvement of the wider nursing and midwifery workforce are given below, and they are followed by a fourth example taken from one of the rare but sentinel cases of child maltreatment that reach the threshold for a statutory SCR.

Trixie and her unborn baby

Trixie, who is a long-term substance misuser, is sixteen weeks pregnant with her first child. She is known to have used cannabis, cocaine and heroin in the past and is now on a methadone (opiate substitution) programme. Her partner, Pete, has a child from a previous relationship. Trixie has recently presented to an emergency nurse practitioner at the local 'walk-in' centre with pain and bruising to her abdomen. The history that was given was that she had tripped and fallen against a pram that was blocking the hallway to her flat. The couple are not currently known to children's social care.

In this case the primary contact with health services is with a specialist midwife who is working within the substance misuse service. Her key role will be one of monitoring the welfare of Trixie and her unborn baby through concordance with the methadone programme and by ensuring that all antenatal healthcare appointments are attended. She will also be able to make an assessment of the couple's preparedness for the birth of the baby, and the continued support that will be available after the baby is born. There will be an expectation that she will liaise with other maternity professionals, as well as the GP and health visitor. This input fits with the notion of secondary prevention; having recognised the risk arising from parental substance misuse, the midwife will seek to support the couple in reducing the risk and promoting protective factors.

Trixie's presentation at the unscheduled care setting should be recognised as resulting from possible domestic violence and abuse. Domestic violence in pregnancy is widely recognised as a key indicator of concern, both for the health and well-being of the woman, and also for the potential of child maltreatment in the future (Lombard and McMillan, 2013). The specialist midwife and the nurse practitioner should liaise and take action to ensure that the risks to the unborn baby are discussed with children's social care, and a child protection referral made accordingly. However as noted by Davies and Ward (2012), a referral to children's social care does not absolve further input from the referrer, and the midwife will continue to provide care and support within the child protection framework as a key member of a core group of professionals working together to reduce the risks and protect the child. These actions reflect tertiary prevention.

Jeremy, a child with cerebral palsy

Jeremy, who is five years of age, has quadriplegic cerebral palsy. He suffers from frequent chest infections and his once occasional fits appear to be increasing. Jeremy's parents have recently separated, and his mother is struggling to cope with Jeremy's care, as well as the parenting needs of her three other children. She has told the GP that 'life is not worth living just now'. The GP has made a referral to primary mental health services as she is concerned that Jeremy's mother may be suffering from clinical depression.

In this case the primary contact with healthcare services is through the children with disabilities team – and in particular the children's community nursing services, who visit the home on a weekly basis. This children's community nurse (CCN), along with the wider healthcare team, have a responsibility to ensure that the needs of all the children in the family are met. This includes making an assessment of the provision of 'safe and effective care', which was noted at the outset of this chapter, which reflects wider safeguarding practice. Linking in with wider family support services, and perhaps respite care for Jeremy may help to prevent child neglect, within what is clearly a difficult time for the family. In addition the mental health worker has a responsibility to make an assessment of the impact of the mother's mental health problems on her ability to parent and to liaise with the CCN regarding the well-being of all the children. The provision of listening visits may be particularly helpful in allowing the mother to express her concerns, and this may in turn reduce the levels of stress in the household.

Sasha, a young person seeking sexual health services

Sasha, who is fourteen years of age, is on the verge of becoming sexually active. Her boyfriend, Jay, who is twenty-one years old, has told her that she needs to 'get herself sorted' to avoid becoming pregnant. She is keen to please him, as he is her first proper boyfriend. He has also been showering her with gifts (like the new mobile phone her parents would not subscribe to) and telling her how special she is. Jay refuses to attend the clinic with her and tells her not to mention his name.

Julie is an experienced sexual health nurse. She prides herself on her ability to form close and supportive relationships with her teenage clients, who in turn demonstrate their trust in the provision of a non-judgemental confidential service. However this scenario is concerning; there are indicators that Sasha may be a young person who is at risk of child sexual exploitation. The key indicators here include the secrecy, the provision of gifts and the age differential (HM Government, 2009). A full assessment should explore these factors and the care provided may include preventative advice on safe and healthy relationships, but also the potential for a referral to children's social care and/or the police.

Evidence from Serious Case Reviews

The evidence drawn from the chronologies that are constructed for SCRs has shown that children and young people who have suffered from grievous or fatal abuse, and their families, may have accessed a range of healthcare services (and patterns of disengagement are important here too) but are not necessarily known to children's social care services (see for example Brandon *et al.*, 2012). Learning and practice improvement as a result of a SCRs is an important aspect of safeguarding and child protection activity (HM Government, 2015). Ensuring 'join up' of professionals and delivering care that is focused on the child within the family are enduring themes in the recommendations that arise from these reviews.

This section of the chapter concludes by providing an example of one child's healthcare journey. The example is taken from a recently published SCR following the untimely and tragic death of an eight year old child from a fatal asthma attack. The child was subject to a child protection plan for emotional abuse in the context of serious and enduring domestic violence and parental substance misuse (Hyde, 2014). (The report concerning Child H, and other published SCRs, can be accessed via the NSPCC SCR website repository.)

Child H

Child H suffered from moderate/severe asthma, eyesight problems, tooth decay, nosebleeds, enuresis and low weight. Father was a substance misuse service user. In the four years leading up to his death, the child was seen by a health visitor, a school nurse, a general practitioner, CCNs, a practice nurse (asthma specialist), three paediatric teams (inpatient and outpatient), an ear, nose and throat team, an orthoptist and emergency department staff. Father was in contact with a substance misuse team.

In this case not all involved professionals were aware of the child protection status of the child or who else was involved in providing health services to the family. This meant that opportunities to intervene were potentially missed and that no one had a complete picture of the daily lived experience of this child and the impact of the parental difficulties on their safety and well-being. The case illustrates the importance of timely and proportionate information-sharing and communication at an intra-agency, as well as an inter-agency level.

Good practice would have been for those providing care to the child and family to have been working more closely together and ensuring that there was a focus on the needs of the child for safe and effective care. This may have included supporting a referral to local domestic violence services. Particular attention should have been given to ensuring that Child H attended his medical appointments and that professionals were satisfied that there was concordance with the therapeutic treatment for his asthma.

Conclusion

This chapter has considered the safeguarding and child protection contribution of the wider nursing and midwifery workforce. This is a role that is supported by policy and guidance. Contemporary curricula for those on all parts of the professional register reflect knowledge, skills and competence in public health as well as in safeguarding children and young people. While safeguarding leadership has tended to be rooted in those with the SCPHN qualification, this must not be at the expense of the provision of support and guidance to the whole family of nursing. The needs of the child are indeed paramount. Care delivery should reflect the centrality and lived experiences of children and young people within their families and be joined up to meet their requirements and to provide for their safety and well-being.

Summary

This chapter has outlined the importance of the safeguarding and child protection contribution of the wider nursing and midwifery workforce. The first section considered the mandate for this responsibility in terms of practice, policy and professional guidance. The second section of the chapter reflected the significance of the healthcare journeys experienced by children and young people (and their parents) and the opportunities that may be presented within these contexts for more proactive and responsive safeguarding children practice across the wider profession.

CHAPTER 6

Small signs, big risks: The importance of early detection

Caroline Bradbury-Jones, University of Birmingham
Julie Taylor, University of Birmingham

Introduction

The role of public health nurses in identifying and responding to children where safeguarding is an issue is well recognised. Also the importance of early detection and intervention is widely accepted. In most instances however the alerting factors are not clear or sudden, but vague, cumulative and insidious. This makes detection and early intervention problematic. In this chapter we use two examples from our own research to show the complexities associated with public health nurses' safeguarding decision-making. We illuminate some of the barriers and challenges associated with their assessments, and the tentative steps they take in weighing up the small signs and big risks.

There is no doubt about the longer-term consequences of child abuse and neglect and living with domestic abuse experience. The importance of early intervention has been emphasised in both research and policy, and it is a key aspect in the role of the public health nurse. Such early intervention is often thought of as being early as possible in a child's life (Allen, 2011b), and given the development needs, vulnerability and reliance on adults of infants this is compelling. Indeed those first 1,001 days, from conception to age two, are seen as critical (Leadsom *et al.*, 2013). However early intervention as soon as risks are identified and early intervention to minimise the effects of harm are very important too.

Safeguarding decision-making would be so much easier if the manifestations of maltreatment were more clear-cut. We know however that, in most situations when making safeguarding assessments regarding families and children, public health nurses are faced with vague, cumulative and insidious alerting risk factors (Appleton, 2011). They are called upon to make tough safeguarding judgements and on the basis of these formulate appropriate responses. Using the mantra 'the safety of the child is paramount' as a yardstick, any concern should be enough to prompt action. But even that is not straightforward. We know from our own practice and from a raft of empirical evidence that in reality thresholds vary and decision-making is complex (Flaherty *et al.,* 2008; Gillingham, 2011; LeBlanc *et al.,* 2012; Mummery, 2002; Stokes and Schmidt, 2012). The purpose of this chapter is to unpick these complexities and to illuminate the relationship between the shifting polymorphic 'small signs' of child maltreatment and their associated 'big risks' in terms of consequences.

We take two of our own studies and use these as case examples to illustrate the challenges that public health nurses face in relation to safeguarding decision-making. Where relevant, we have used data from the studies to enliven the discussion and highlight how public health nurses talk about such issues. We have chosen these particular studies because they not only focused on the role of public health nurses but also explored different safeguarding angles. Combined, they reflect different contexts and possibilities with which it is hoped most public health nurses can identify. The studies are: Dental neglect study (Bradbury-Jones *et al.,* 2013); and Domestic abuse study (Bradbury-Jones *et al.,* 2014; Taylor *et al.,* 2013) (see Table 6.1 for details).

Study 1: Dental neglect

Study 1 context

Child neglect is a significant issue in terms of prevalence and severity and there is indubitable evidence that it is harmful to children (Lazenbatt *et al.,* 2012). A range of adverse health outcomes causally related to neglect is demonstrated significantly in both prospective and retrospective studies (Norman *et al.,* 2012). Abused and neglected children have been found to have higher levels of tooth decay than the general population (Valencia-Rojas *et al.,* 2008). Parents or carers who persistently fail to obtain dental treatment for their child's tooth decay are an alerting feature that should prompt practitioners to consider neglect (National Collaborating Centre for Women's and Children's Health, 2009). Dental neglect may exist in isolation, but this is rare and it is recognised that untreated dental disease is an indicator of broader child neglect (Harris *et al.,* 2009; Balmer *et al.,* 2010).

Before commencing the study, we knew from previous work that public health nurses use dental neglect as a proxy indicator of broader neglect in children (Taylor *et al.,* 2009). However at the time the question of what public health nurses actually do to assess for dental neglect was unclear. We also understood from the work of Daniel *et al.* (2011) that there is considerable variation in health professionals' perceptions of thresholds of neglect. With these things in mind, we investigated how public health nurses made assessments of dental neglect and the threshold levels of neglect that alerted them to a child protection concern.

Public health nurses' assessments in Study 1

The principal means of assessment of dental neglect described by the public health nurses in this study was through discussion: for

Table 6.1 Details of the two studies.

Focus of study	Study details	Key findings	References
Study 1: Dental neglect	In 2011/12 we undertook a study in Scotland to investigate public health nurses' role in assessing oral health in preschool children in relation to dental neglect. Sixteen public health nurses were interviewed to elicit information regarding how they assessed the oral health of children and the thresholds of dental caries they used that alerted them to a child protection concern.	• Public health nurses assess oral health through proxy measures, opportunistic observation and through discussion with parents. • Dental neglect is rarely an isolated issue that leads on its own to child protection referral. • Threshold levels for child protection intervention are untreated dental caries or significant dental pain. • Barriers to early detection and intervention are that dental neglect may be 'unseen' and 'unspoken'.	Bradbury-Jones *et al.* (2013)
Study 2: Domestic abuse	This two-phase, qualitative study undertaken in Scotland in 2011 investigated health professionals' beliefs about domestic abuse and the issue of disclosure. In phase one, twenty-nine health professionals were recruited from two health boards (regions): midwives n=11; health visitors (public health nurses) n=16; general practitioners/family physicians n=2. They were interviewed to elicit their beliefs about domestic abuse. In the second phase, three focus group interviews were undertaken with fourteen women with domestic abuse experiences, comprising: group 1 n=4; group 2 n=7; group 3 n=3.	• Public health nurses and abused women do not always share the same views about domestic abuse. For example, women want to be asked about abuse but many health professionals — including public health nurses — do not feel confident or comfortable discussing the issue. • Many women fail to recognise their experiences as abusive. • In combination, these issues delay or hamper opportunities for disclosure, early intervention, support and safety planning.	Bradbury-Jones *et al.* (2014); Taylor *et al.* (2013)

example, talking to parents about dental hygiene, dietary habits, and registration with a dentist. Out of the sixteen public health nurses who took part, most (n=10) mentioned that they did not routinely look in a child's mouth (unless asked to do so by the parent/carer). Most observations of a child's teeth were opportunistic, rather than a planned activity. As explained by the following public health nurses, waiting for a child to laugh or smile provided an ideal opportunity:

> 'I would just look at their teeth as I was chatting to the children.'

> 'Just a smile … a smile of a child you can sometimes see things aren't as they should be.'

When describing their reticence about looking directly into a child's mouth, some public health nurses raised the interesting point that the mouth is a very private area and to explicitly request to look in another person's mouth can be intrusive. But, for most, direct observation was deemed simply to be beyond their sphere of practice:

> 'I wouldn't say it's my role to look in a child's mouth.'

> 'No never, never because I wouldn't know what I was looking for.'

The public health nurses stated that they become alert to the need for targeted support in relation to dental neglect when faced with two broad indicators: social issues, and concerns about dental health. Social determinants such as homelessness, poor housing, domestic abuse and parental substance misuse were the main alerting issues. Two public health nurses explained what they look for in their dental health assessments. The things that 'worry' them were:

> 'You're looking at the risk factors … whether the parents are sub-stance misusers, victims of domestic abuse, sexual abuse and, just, their own family history.'

> 'The sort of things that would worry me particularly would be rela-tionship issues, mental health, poor social circumstances in a damp house or overcrowding.'

It is clear that the assessments of the public health nurses in the study involved close consideration of the contextual issues associ-ated with potential dental neglect. Targeted support comprised provision of additional resources to promote dental health (such as toothbrushes) and referral to dental services.

We were interested in thresholds and the level at which they would be prompted into the need for child protection intervention. There were two key indicators: a child suffering from untreated dental caries or significant dental pain (n=10), and parents failing to take their child for dental care after being advised to do so (n=7). This was in line with the indicators of neglect discussed earlier (Harris *et al.*, 2009; Balmer *et al.*, 2010) and shows congruence between the public health nurses' practice and best practice guidelines. However a recurrent theme throughout the study was the complexity of assessment – a finding that supports earlier research (Appleton and Cowley, 2008a). According to the public health nurses who took part, dental neglect is rarely an isolated issue; it is invariably part of a mosaic of problems associated with a neglected child. One public health nurse described this as 'an overall picture of neglect'.

Key lessons learned from Study 1
The study highlighted an endemic lack of communication between dental services and public health nurses. Public health nurses tended to be reliant on parental reporting of attendance at dental services and the outcomes for children. This made ongoing assessments and decision-making problematic, particularly where there were concerns about dental neglect. The participants did not see dental neglect as an indication of potential wider neglect and may have missed an opportunity for early detection. The public health nurses in the study were quite simply not equipped with sufficient information to allow for holistic assessments and a gap in the care pathway was identified.

A striking issue – and one to which will be returned to – was the perceived sensitivity of the issue and fear among many public health nurses of getting things wrong. Appleton and Cowley (2008a) refer to the notion of 'gauging' as part of the assessment process – an intricate and delicate weighing up of the nuanced aspects of a relationship. Similarly in our study we found that a careful balancing was required in order to make appropriate assessments of a child's health and to maintain positive relationships with parents/carers. The study showed how public health nurses tread very carefully:

'It's trying to do it a bit more subtly, because you want to see them again. You don't want them to say, "I'm not going to see her again".'

'It's really difficult because … no one has to let me in [to their house],
no one has to uptake that service, they can say no.'

Later in the chapter we will discuss the complexities of protecting
children in the here and now, while still protecting future relationships with families.

Study 2: Domestic abuse

Study 2 context

For the purpose of this study, domestic abuse was defined as:

> Any incident or pattern of incidents of controlling, coercive, threatening
> behaviour, violence or abuse between those aged 16 or over who are or
> have been intimate partners or family members regardless of gender
> or sexuality. The abuse can encompass but is not limited to: psycho-
> logical, physical, sexual, financial [or] emotional (Home Office, 2012).

As a research team we use this particular definition because it captures a range of different types of abuse and it also reflects the fact that
domestic abuse occurs in many relationship configurations: it is not only
men who are violent to women. However in the domestic abuse study
we focused on the experiences of abused women.

Before commencing this study we already knew that abused women
are reluctant to disclose (Ahmad et al., 2009; Feder et al., 2009) and that
more than 20% will never tell anyone about it (Spangaro et al., 2011).
One of the reasons that women do not discuss their abuse was that they
worry about removal of children (Peckover, 2003; Montalvo-Liendo et al.,
2009). Although in most cases this fear is completely unjustified, there is
increasing evidence about the long-term negative impact upon children
exposed to domestic abuse (Humphreys et al., 2008; Peckover, 2003),
which in the UK has informed current policy regarding domestic abuse
(CAADA, 2014; NICE, 2014b).

In this study we were also interested in health professionals' beliefs
about domestic abuse and the relationship these have with the issue of
disclosure. Sixteen public health nurses took part (see Table 6.1). We
looked into many different aspects of their beliefs (such as who is likely
to experience abuse; its severity; likely consequences) as well as their
beliefs about the impact of abuse on children and that is what we focus
upon here.

Public health nurses' assessments in Study 2

It is known that health visitors make complex assessments based
on multiple factors (Appleton and Cowley, 2008a) and this was

evident in Study 2 (as also in Study 1). When talking about the families with whom they had been involved, rarely did domestic abuse present as a discreet, one-off event. Almost invariably it was part of a myriad of other presenting issues, which made assessments and response a challenge. As captured in the words of the public health nurse here, alcohol, drugs and mental health issues were almost always part of the contextual picture when discussing their clients:

> 'She did have an alcohol problem and there was a lot of stuff going on there and she had kind of … there was a lot of quite, you know, neglect of the children going on and that was quite obvious and neglect of herself as well.'

> 'I was working with the family for quite a few years and she was actually schizophrenic and she was going through a particularly difficult time … I wanted to find out what was making her mental health particularly bad at this time and she disclosed that her partner had been abusing her.'

This chapter is concerned with the complexity of assessments around safeguarding and what has been termed the 'small signs'. So in their assessments, it was apparent that the public health nurses in Study 2 were identifying the multiplicity of issues associated with domestic abuse (such as alcohol and mental health issues) and piecing them together to form a mosaic of alerting signs.

As discussed earlier, we were particularly interested in public health nurses' beliefs about domestic abuse and risks to any children exposed to it. Without exception public health nurses were aware of the negative impact of domestic abuse and provided some stark illustrations in support of their concerns:

> 'I've got a family at the moment, recently the father tried to burn the house down with the mother and the youngest child inside and this child now is having counselling. He's at nursery. He's shouting "Fire, Fire" in the playhouse and chucking the dollies out of the window because he's trying to re-enact it.'

One public health nurse was particularly categorical about risks to children:

'Now where there's domestic abuse – domestic violence – that's a child protection issue,'

Thus the public health nurses in the study were aware of the negative impacts of domestic abuse on any children in the household. However their assessments and early interventions were complicated by the reluctance of many mothers to acknowledge the impact that the abuse might have on their children:

'What we often hear is: "My partner wouldn't harm the baby" and even when you categorically state to them "That may be the case but they can be accidentally harmed and then there's the emotional impact. You cannot spare the child or the baby from that".'

One of the reasons that women do not discuss their abuse is that they worry about removal of children. In line with the work of Peckover (2003) and Montalvo-Liendo *et al.* (2009) presented earlier, public health nurses are aware of the guilt, shame and fear that abused women feel and the significant lengths they go to in order to protect their children. Another important reason for non-disclosure is that women may not identify their experiences as abusive. One of the abused women in the study explained:

'You have to come to the stage that you have realised that you are being abused, I mean I never had black eyes or anything, so I had nothing on the outside, but it is in here that I cried [gesturing to heart]. See if you don't know that you are being abused you cannot tell somebody that you are being abused.'

When exploring the issue of non-disclosure, one of the public health nurses described her means of supporting a woman to 'see' the abuse:

'She said: "Well, he's very controlling and he always puts me down, whatever I ask the child to do, he says they don't need to do it" ... and I asked about physical violence and she said there was no physical violence but ... when we went back over what was happening I was saying: "Well that sounds like abuse to me".'

Key lessons learned from Study 2

As already discussed, domestic abuse is a stigmatised taboo issue (Buck and Collins, 2007) and women do not always get the support they seek when they disclose (Peckover, 2003). Thus in order to facilitate disclosure, building supportive relationships is important and particularly those that pave the way for open discussions about abuse (Feder *et al.*, 2006; Bradbury-Jones *et al.*, 2014). The dental neglect study highlighted how the public health nurses valued their relationships with families, and, as illustrated in the excerpt below, this was echoed in the domestic abuse study, where the established relationship had seemingly facilitated disclosure:

> 'We had built up a relationship over a year … I didn't ask about domestic violence then and she didn't … I don't know whether she felt she had built up a relationship with me … I remember she looked as though she was unwell, as if she had cold symptoms and was miserable and then she just started crying and told me that she couldn't go home and that's when I started exploring what had been going on.'

In line with previous researchers (Appleton and Cowley, 2008a) in the dental neglect study we found that there was a perceived need among public health nurses to tread carefully in order to protect their relationships with the client/family. Again this was also present in the domestic abuse study:

> 'I don't ask them right out if they're a victim of domestic abuse but I ask them about, you know, was the baby planned, are you happy and your husband, how's your partner feeling about it? It's up to your perception and your judgement … we make judgements that may be presumptions rather than evidence and I still find … I don't find it easy … you don't want to offend people … and you're not going to have a relationship with them if you have offended them …. it's hard to get the balance.'

For more than a decade a substantial body of evidence has amassed to show that most women find it acceptable to be asked about domestic abuse (Bacchus *et al.*, 2002; Taket *et al.*, 2003; Keeling and Birch, 2004; Feder *et al.*, 2009). Over the same period of time, studies have shown how many health professionals are reluctant to discuss the issue (Mezey *et al.*, 2003; Lazenbatt *et al.*, 2009; Montalvo-Liendo, 2009; Beynon *et al.*, 2012). The domestic abuse study provided recent evidence to support this (Bradbury-Jones *et al.*, 2014; Taylor *et al.*, 2013). The public health nurse participants mentioned their fear of causing offence and the risk of ruined relationships. But we know of the serious consequences of domestic abuse for children and the need for early intervention (CAADA, 2014; NICE, 2014b). So this does beg the question: what about the risks of not discussing the issue and the risks to children of continued exposure to domestic abuse?

Study 2 highlighted the complexity of working with families where domestic abuse is an issue. Public health nurses are called upon to make judgements regarding potential existence of abuse, how to broach the issue, likely risk, safeguarding and safety planning. Yet all this is in the context of an array of factors associated with domestic abuse, meaning that assessments are most often complicated by women's reluctance to disclose abuse, their lack of awareness of the abusive nature of their relationship, or public health nurses' concern about getting things wrong. All these issues make for complex assessments and decision-making. Importantly they impact on the ability to identify domestic abuse early, so that support and appropriate referral can take place.

Conclusion

In the two studies presented in this chapter, we have highlighted the crucial safeguarding role of public health nurses. In study 1, we showed how their accurate timely assessment of children for dental neglect meant that they were potential catalysts in securing a child's overall safety and well-being. It was clear that dental neglect was taken seriously by public health nurses, but it was not easily assessed or well defined in terms of thresholds. In the second study we noted that public health nurses were attuned to the impact of domestic abuse on children and they regarded it as a safeguarding issue. Across both of these studies, what we could term the 'immediacy versus longevity' narrative was strong. Public health nurses trod carefully because they did not want to offend (by requesting to look in a child's mouth for example, or by asking about abuse within personal relationships). In comparison to many health professionals, public health nurses have relatively long-term relationships with families, and both studies provided evidence of a desire to protect these relationships. To cause offence put relationships in jeopardy and threatened subsequent contact with a family (Appleton and Cowley, 2008a).

Public health nurses have a critical role in protecting children, and early detection of and response to (potential) harm is critical. There are however a number of inherent tensions. The dynamic of dealing with the here and now, while protecting future contacts, adds a complexity to public health nurses' assessments. In many respects the 'big risks' that feature in the title of this chapter and the discussion within it refer not only to risks to children (and abused women), but also to the perceived risks among many public health nurses, of damaged relationships. But what does all this mean for safeguarding decision-making? Does an eye to the future and protection of long-term relationships threaten the perceived need to act immediately? Or does leaving the door open to future contact actually mean greater, longer-term protection for children? This could be a question worthy of empirical investigation.

Summary

Public health nurses play a crucial safeguarding role, but this chapter has highlighted the multiplicity of interrelated contextual factors that might compound early detection and intervention. Examples from our empirical work on abuse, neglect and domestic abuse illustrated the challenges. In support of previous researchers, we have highlighted a balancing act undertaken by public health nurses to protect children while simultaneously protecting their relationships with families. The challenge is that 'small signs' are rarely singular – they are multiple and complex. So, whether dental neglect or domestic abuse, assessments are challenging. Yet both of these issues hold considerable risks for children, and early detection and intervention are necessary. In this chapter we have contributed to the debate about the impact that complex assessments have for public health nurses' intervention with high risk families, and suggest that further research is required in this area.

CHAPTER 7

Safeguarding services in NHS acute hospitals: The challenge of leadership

Suzanne Smith, Assistant Director of Nursing (Safeguarding), UK

Introduction

The visibility and location of safeguarding leadership within the culturally different areas of acute and community provision are an important consideration in the ever-shifting landscape and reform of the NHS in England. Changes to commissioning and provider arrangements have brought a change to the location and development of safeguarding lead roles including statutory named and designated roles and emergent non-statutory positions. These changes present a challenge to the potential for safeguarding leads to remain clinically connected. Within the acute sector, the visibility of safeguarding is a constant challenge with a real and apparent disconnect between safeguarding and the patient safety and quality agendas, and a focus on technical solutions and knowledge frameworks which do not easily lend themselves to safeguarding practice. This chapter examines the implications for safeguarding leads in acute organisations, the need for safeguarding to be strategically located throughout the three key domains of quality – clinical effectiveness, patient safety and patient experience – and for the connection to be made with these domains and clinical practice.

Safeguarding Children and the NHS context

Safeguarding children and adults at risk is recognised as a fundamental part of core business within primary care and community health service provision (HM Government, 2015; NHS Commissioning Board, 2013; DH, 2000). Safeguarding children has always been recognised as a key element among health visiting and school health services, and the focus of the development and leadership of safeguarding children services within the NHS has traditionally been on these community services. Arguably this focus has resulted in the potential and impact of safeguarding services within secondary care being hidden. The movement of community nursing services in the ever-shifting landscape of the NHS has created additional challenges, whether those services be part of social enterprise arrangements or acute service provider arrangements as well as the imminent move to local authority provision.

In April 2013 the NHS in England underwent major reform with the establishment of Clinical Commissioning Groups (CCGs) with responsibility for commissioning most local healthcare services. At the same time local authorities were given responsibility for commissioning most public health services.

Child protection is now increasingly being understood within a public health framework (Gilbert *et al.*, 2008; Barlow and Calam, 2011; Daniel *et al.* 2011, pp. 143–60; Peckover and Smith, 2011) in which upstream approaches that focus on early intervention and prevention are emphasised and performance measured. The safeguarding adult agenda is following similar lines with the publication of the Francis report (2013) and *Winterbourne View Hospital: A Serious Case Review* (Flynn, 2012) as well as the Care Act 2014, the bulk of which was implemented in April 2015. The NHS Commissioning Board (2013) is clear that NHS accountability and responsibility for safeguarding are not altered by the reform of the NHS:

> NHS organisations – whether as commissioners or providers of NHS funded care – must demonstrate strong local leadership, work as committed partners and invest in effective co-ordination and robust quality assurance of safeguarding arrangements (NHS Commissioning Board (2013, p. 8).

Within the NHS, named and designated professionals in child protection/safeguarding children are the key personnel leading safeguarding services both strategically and operationally within commissioning and provider organisations. Their role is defined in statutory guidance (HM Government, 2015) and the structures within which they operate has been defined by the NHS Commissioning Board (2013). Designated nurses are expected to take a strategic lead on all aspects of safeguarding children within the health economy, while named professionals are tasked with promoting good practice and providing advice for professionals in their organisation. According to the NHS Commissioning Board (2013) designated nurses are likely to be located within commissioning organisations (although designated doctors may be located in acute care provision), and named professionals are largely, but not exclusively found within provider organisations. Anecdotal evidence suggests that the safeguarding adult role is sometimes combined with the traditional role of the named and designated safeguarding children roles. The different skill sets and knowledge base required are often not clarified.

Safety, safeguarding and risk management: identifying the disconnect

The challenge to embed and lead safeguarding children and adult services within acute hospital settings in the NHS has always encountered an essential difficulty in determining where the speciality sits within the much broader range of services. The mantra is often quoted that 'safeguarding is everybody's business', and this ethos is certainly inherent within statutory guidance (HM Government, 2015; DH, 2000). How well that is embraced within different surgical, medical and diagnostic specialities is not however well understood.

Despite the fact that the Children Act 1989 defines a child as someone who has not yet reached their eighteenth birthday, named nurses and midwives who work in acute settings will be familiar with the comment that 'we don't work with children' from medical and nursing staff in adult areas who treat and care for young people from sixteen years of age. Similarly paediatricians and children's nurses may not appreciate the requirement for them to attend safeguarding adult training even though they interact with adult parents of their patients on a daily basis. This presents a cultural barrier to those leading safeguarding children and adult services in the delivery of their safeguarding strategy. This is probably more prevalent in acute services than in community services and primary care. The difference in culture between primary and secondary healthcare remains almost palpable, for which a different approach and leadership style may be required. The need for a clear safeguarding leadership is ever growing especially in the current context where integrated care and adoption of community services within traditionally acute service providers become the norm (Barker, 2014; West *et al.*, 2014).

Leading safeguarding children and adult services within an acute hospital setting requires a process of engagement, of embracing opportunities, of educating, supporting and empowering staff to 'do' the business of safeguarding rather than it being 'done' to them, and in this sense the challenge is similar in both hospital and community settings. The starting point however and the rate of progress are likely to be different. There is little point in doing a word search for 'safeguarding' in documents such as the Francis report (2013), Keogh review (2013) or National Advisory Group on Patient Safety review (National Advisory Group on the Safety of Patients in England, 2013) as safeguarding is not specifically mentioned as a concept. Yet it is crucial to use the opportunity of such publications to demonstrate how they embrace the protection and safety of patients from harm, including harm caused by abuse.

Literature regarding patient safety is widely available with a strong focus on the importance of communication, feedback loops, confidential reporting and organisational learning (Francis, 2013; Keogh, 2013; National Advisory Group on the Safety of Patients in England, 2013; Vincent, 2010). Literature on safeguarding children very much reflects the same issues and is especially prevalent in biannual reports on SCRs (Brandon *et al.*, 2012) and in the Munro review (Munro, 2011). However there is an apparent disconnect between patient safety literature and safeguarding literature, which may be a reflection of how safeguarding is seen, through a hospital lens, as something that is essentially discrete, highly specialised and community focused. It may also be the case that the connection between safeguarding and patient safety is not viewed as relevant by community staff.

Contemporary discourses focusing on safeguarding children within the NHS in England highlight the deep-rooted challenges in balancing assessment and decision-making with management of risk and minimising uncertainty (Hanlon *et al.*, 2005; Munro, 2011; Peckover *et al.*, 2013). The phenomenon of child abuse is in itself socially constructed without fixed or permanent boundaries, making precise definition impossible (Parton *et al.*, 1997). The interaction between the complex multifaceted layers of strengths and needs that may feature within a family and may be influenced to different degrees by environmental factors will vary with each case. Precise prediction is therefore an unrealistic goal and an unlikely achievement. Despite organisational objectives to manage risk and minimise uncertainty, professionals working in the field of safeguarding children have to tolerate a level of uncertainty (Munro, 2011). Even technological and algorithmic protocols designed to minimise uncertainty are shown to be unhelpful when dealing with value-sensitive problems (Smith, 2010; White and Stancombe, 2003; Taylor and White, 2000).

The same challenges apply as much to the safeguarding adult agenda. This can lead to frustration in a technologically dominated acute medical environment. Safeguarding leads may find themselves persuaded to search for risk assessment tools and technological solutions such as creating flags on hospital systems or undertaking universal screening, despite the lack of evidence of any impact on child and family outcomes, concerns about diverting clinical attention from other risk indicators and worries that parents and children will be deterred from attending unscheduled care settings (Woodman and Gilbert, 2013: Jewkes, 2013; Woodman *et al.*, 2008, 2010; Hawkes, 2012).

The technical response to solving complex and dynamic social and human interaction problems proves attractive in the NHS as much to the nursing profession as it does to the medical profession. Framing the discourse about assessment and decision-making in safeguarding is the growing tension within the NHS about how information and knowledge should be prioritised. Kelly and Symonds (2003) describe the 'identity crises' that has developed as nurses have sought 'professional prestige' by privileging the medical profession's use of science over caring skills. The process of assessment in any medically focused healthcare setting can arguably be seen as a means of hypothetico-deduction, the aim of which is to try and reduce risk. Kelly and Symonds (2003, p. 114) emphasise: ' "powerful" interpretations of governmentality tended to devalue nursing care in favour of developing technological interventions which were the province of the medical profession'.

Lam (2000) contests that the dominant knowledge type depends on the type of organisation. She identifies an alliance between 'embrained knowledge' and 'professional bureaucracy', where highly skilled professionals acquire knowledge through formal education and training and are governed by professional bodies. This description could be applied to a variety of professions including medicine and nursing. Lam (2000, p. 492-3) goes on to identify 'encoded knowledge' typified as 'knowledge that is codified, explicit and collective, which facilitates organisational control and does not capture individual skill, judgement or tacit knowledge'. Encoded knowledge is closely associated with a 'machine bureaucracy', features of which are described as:

> a clear division of labour and specialisation, close supervision, and continuous efforts to codify knowledge and skills to reduce uncertainty (and variation), and an emphasis on managerially generated rules, monitoring procedures and performance standards. A machine bureaucracy tries to minimise the use of tacit knowledge, and corrects mistakes through performance monitoring (Flynn, 2002, p. 167).

Munro (2011) highlights the dangers of what translates to encoded over embrained knowledge for social workers in their child protection work and comments: 'high levels of prescription have also hampered the profession's ability to take responsibility for developing its own knowledge and skills' (Munro, 2011, p. 8).

The question arises as to the degree this migration from professional to machine bureaucracy, such as the persistent search and production of risk assessment indicators and numeric risk-based tools, has happened or is happening in the NHS. The answer to such a question outlines the scale of the challenge for the safeguarding named nurses, midwives, heads of safeguarding and executive safeguarding leads in hospital trusts.

Measuring quality and developing knowledge

The ever-increasing numbers of performance indicators and appraisal systems lend some support to the notion that the dominant knowledge type within the NHS is increasingly framed by encoded knowledge and a machine bureaucracy represented by the scheme of clinical governance (Ruston, 2006; Flynn, 2002). This can be illustrated by comparing a nursing record in the 1980s, which consisted of a simple problem-solving process underpinned by an assessment of the 'Activities of Daily Living' (Roper *et al.*, 1996), with a typical nursing record in the twenty-first century, which includes numerous risk assessment scoring tools for many different areas of care. It could be argued that this is an example of how nursing practice has embraced a bureaucracy that minimises the use of tacit knowledge in the search to counter error and avoid blame.

The National Advisory Group on the Safety of Patients in England (2013) highlights the danger of this response in its report following the findings of the Francis enquiry into Mid Staffordshire NHS Trust (Francis, 2013). The bold statement is presented as a headline: 'Incorrect priorities do damage'. The report goes on to highlight:

> In some organisations, in the face of the prime directive, 'the needs of the patient come first', goals of (a) hitting targets and (b) reducing costs have taken centre stage ... Under such conditions organisations can hit the target, but miss the point (National Advisory Group on the Safety of Patients in England, 2013, p. 8).

The National Advisory Group on the Safety of Patients in England (2013) acknowledges the importance of quantitative targets but warns that they should be used with caution, especially financial targets. It draws attention to the fact that the albeit unintended outcome of such a narrow focus is that the patient becomes invisible and the target of good patient care is missed. The importance of learning and knowledge sharing as opposed to pure data sharing is emphasised in the report.

The same theme was picked up by Munro in 2011. Quoting Reder and Duncan (2003), Munro (2011) highlights that sharing information was not about shifting data from one computer to another but required an impact on knowledge and understanding from the people in receipt of the information in order for it to make a difference. However effective communication is not just a matter of moving a datum from one computer to another. She quotes Reder and Duncan (2003), who emphasise that effective communication is 'the process by which information is transferred from one person to another and is understood by them' (Reder and Duncan, 2003, p. 148).

Nevertheless the preoccupation of inspectorates and policymakers with measurable indicators such as numbers of Common Assessment Framework forms completed remains a challenge, because positive outcomes in safeguarding cannot always be so easily counted and accurately identified (White *et al.*, 2015).

A wider framework for measuring quality in the secondary care NHS sector is provided by Lord Darzi (DH, 2008), whose definition of quality for the NHS is well known and can be summarised as:

- safety (avoiding harm from the care that is intended to help);
- effectiveness (aligning care with science and ensuring efficiency);
- patient experience (including patient-centredness, timeliness and equity) (National Advisory Group on the Safety of Patients in England, 2013, p. 11).

A safeguarding strategy in an acute healthcare setting is likely to be better aligned to organisational objectives if these three key areas are reflected. The fact that the Francis (2013), Keogh (2013) and National Advisory Group on the Safety of Patients in England (2013) reports are not cross-referenced with safeguarding literature and reports such as the Munro (2011) report should not be a reason why the ethos expressed in all the reports cannot form the backbone of the safeguarding strategy. An example might be consideration of how lessons from SCRs are disseminated and learned.

Safety, safeguarding and quality in hospital settings
Making the connection
The acute healthcare setting will address risk management and learning lessons as part of its quality strategy. The management of error and neglect is now a fundamental part of the culture of secondary care and has heightened attention following the Francis report (2013) and the *Winterbourne View Hospital: A Serious Case Review* (Flynn, 2012). The patient safety approach is founded on human factors and the position that humans will make errors. The response to

error and the reaction to wilful misconduct should be different. The commentary on this in the National Advisory Group on the Safety of Patients in England (2013) and in Munro (2011) are similar, and they focus on the fact that well-intentioned people will make mistakes or are involved in systems that have failed around them. The organisational response should be supportive rather than punitive so that a culture of openness in reporting mistakes and system failures in order to learn can be addressed. Enhancing congruency between patient safety and safeguarding discourse includes using the quality framework and patient safety mechanisms for disseminating findings from clinical incidents and for distributing reports from SCRs, thus strengthening at operational and strategic level the alignment between the safeguarding and patient safety and quality agendas.

The need to design innovative systems that 'fit' with the culture of the acute hospital is a necessary part of embedding safeguarding within the organisation and ensuring an element of 'future proofing'. As Munro (2011) highlights:

> Managers ... exercise leadership to challenge and bring about change and improvement focused on securing a better future.... Leadership is much more than the authority of key figureheads. Leadership should be valued and encouraged at all levels (Munro, 2011, pp. 106–7).

Collective leadership
Although to some the culture of the acute hospital setting may seem impregnable, it is co-created by all the people in the organisation. In common with all NHS health and social care and public health settings, it is dynamic and 'the way we do things around here' as a set of shared assumptions shifts with changes of governments, executives and workforce. West *et al.* (2014) emphasise the need for collective leadership:

> At a time when there is growing interest in integrated care and partnership working between the NHS, local authorities and third sector organisations, collective leadership in local health systems has never been more important or necessary (West *et al.*, 2014, p. 2).

This current developing landscape presents an opportunity for safeguarding leads in acute trusts to shape the emerging culture of their organisations. Collective leadership demands that everyone takes responsibility for the success of their organisation rather than their particular work area. Wherever the expertise and motivation sits within the organisation is where the allocation of leadership will occur, creating a culture across the whole system that crosses professional and organisational boundaries (West *et al.*, 2014).

Leadership, visibility and clinical connectedness
The visibility of safeguarding must be part of this, with safeguarding leads reporting directly to executive board representatives. The importance of ensuring safeguarding is part of the discourse of quality is an essential part of this recognition and opportunity. The National Advisory Group on the Safety of Patients in England (2013) stresses this in its recommendations and calls for 'quality of care in general and patient safety in particular' to be the top priority for all leaders concerned with NHS healthcare (National Advisory Group on the Safety of Patients in England, 2013, p. 15). In addition to ensuring alignment at a strategic level, safeguarding leads have to translate the vision into agreed clear objectives which are distinct, recognisable and share alignment from frontline staff to the board (Locke and Latham, 2013).

In their study focusing on the interface between health and social care around safeguarding children, White *et al.* (2015) challenge the notion of leadership as an architectural linear process espoused by Kotter (1995). They support the view of Weick (1995), who describes the demands on leaders and organisational design as being dynamic and emergent, spontaneous and organic. White *et al.* (2015) support the call for combining known quantitative techniques with qualitative methodology in order to lead change. This includes the need to embrace proven design methods such as prototyping and the use of ethnographic methods to gain a rich understanding of the complex realities of even mundane practices.

White *et al.* (2015) conclude that persistence, resilience and vigilance from the safeguarding leadership and executive teams are crucial. These qualities should frame essential processes of user-centred design, piloting and a thorough engagement with everyday practices and emerging patterns. Such processes require being in touch and involved with the practitioners they support. A new online referral form is given as an example by White *et al.* (2015) of how nursing and medical professionals design and test a form, under the leadership of the safeguarding professionals, that fits the established culture of the trust. The form incorporates the Situation, Background, Assessment, Recommendation (SBAR) communication tool from the NHS Institute for Innovation and Improvement (2008), which is a well-embedded patient safety tool. The results are described as being positive with appreciation of the improved clarity of information by children's social care departments.

The notion of safeguarding leaders being connected and in touch with everyday practice has resonance with the leadership ideals put forward by the National Advisory Group on the Safety of Patients in England (2013) and West *et al.* (2014). There is an unequivocal call for leaders to 'remain connected' with those for whom they are responsible and to have 'first-hand knowledge of the reality of the system at the front line' (National Advisory Group on the Safety of Patients in England, 2013, p. 15). The need for succession planning by inspiring and developing new leaders in the NHS is also a crucial part of the leadership commentary in current and contemporary, NHS-focused reports. This is seen as fundamental to improvement, learning and cultural change.

The reorganisation of the NHS in recent years has arguably made the notion of clinical connectedness something of a challenge. The beginning of the commissioner/provider split was heralded by the Department of Health (DH, 2004) and began in April 2005. Prior to this designated nurses for safeguarding children often managed a team of named nurses. Their daily proximity to the challenges presented on the frontline of practice was apparent as they took the calls, gave supervision and advised practitioners. Some designated nurses combined their role with that of nurse consultant and would also co-manage cases with practitioners as part of their clinical role.

Following April 2005 many designated nurses moved into the commissioning arm of Primary Care Trusts and later became part of CCGs with no direct management of named nurses, many of whom became employees of local acute trusts or social enterprise organisations. The ability for designated nurses to remain clinically connected became more of a challenge despite the overall intention of the new arrangements being to promote clinical engagement. Anecdotal evidence suggests some designated nurses had the safeguarding adult role added to their safeguarding children role without any assessment of appropriate knowledge and competency and little consideration of the legal and operational differences between the two roles.

A unique position developed whereby designated nurses working with named nurses was seen as a conflict of interests. Some named nurse teams then found themselves managed by people without the level of knowledge and expertise in safeguarding as held by the designated nurses. Both posts remain as statutory requirements under *Working Together to Safeguard Children* (HM Government, 2015).

Added to the mix has been the growth in acute trusts of 'heads of safeguarding for adults and children', who report directly to the executive board leads for safeguarding and who carry neither named nor designated status. These posts are not statutory and are often not included in safeguarding fora attended by designated nurses, making the need for extremely robust links between designated nurses and heads of safeguarding in provider settings. This raises questions about how the experience and expertise of senior non-statutory post holders, some of whom, like the author, have been designated nurses in the past, can be harnessed and shared in a positive, patient-focused manner.

As the reformed NHS, including the newly created NHS England, becomes embedded the challenge will be the extent to which the traditional safeguarding leadership structure can continue to claim to have what the National Advisory Group on the Safety of Patients in England (2013, p.15) refers to as 'first-hand reality of the system at the front line'. Over time, if CCGs and NHS England adopt a recruitment strategy that demands commissioning experience, that connection to the frontline stands a high risk of becoming eroded. Conversely clinical connectedness is preserved in other senior non-statutory positions. The challenge is ensuring that relationships are such that the two statutory and non-statutory elements serve each other and that pathways are created to facilitate and maintain this.

Safeguarding leads – whether holders of statutory posts, heads of safeguarding or nurse managers/executives with a safeguarding lead responsibility – should equip themselves with the language, knowledge and skills to position themselves as part of the collective leadership that will form the bedrock of the changing acute culture as it embraces integrated care and more outward-facing partnership working. Proximity, connection and knowledge of practice on the frontline must be preserved as the NHS continues to shift and move. This is essential to maintain a safeguarding voice in the developing culture as the National Advisory Group on the Safety of Patients in England (2013) states:

> Culture change and continual improvement come from what leaders do, through their commitment, encouragement, compassion and modelling of appropriate behaviours (National Advisory Group on the Safety of Patients in England (2013, p. 15)).

Conclusion

Safeguarding children and adult leads within the acute hospital trust setting face challenges of hospital culture and recognition of the importance of safeguarding as part of core business. Effective leadership includes becoming part of the culture and is an essential factor to ensure safeguarding children and adults at risk is recognised as a priority rather than imposing a language and ethos that, although theoretically completely aligned, is treated even in the literature as being something separate. The safeguarding children and adult strategy has to be clearly aligned to quality including patient safety, patient experience and clinical effectiveness from the objectives of the safeguarding team through to the corporate objectives of the board. Innovation should be explored as an emergent and evolutionary design process that fits with the changing culture of the organisation. There is a need to weigh the balance of risk with the endless search for technological solutions that cannot inform or predict the complexities of human behaviour and to ensure that professionals within the acute sector are supported and empowered to make clinical decisions rooted in evidence-based knowledge.

CHAPTER 8

Child protection, public health and nursing: Final thoughts

Jane V. Appleton, Oxford Brookes University
Sue Peckover, Sheffield Hallam University

Introduction

This chapter will review and summarise critically the key themes emerging from the previous chapters, which in different ways have all highlighted the important role that nurses have in prevention and early identification work with children, young people and their families as well as their protection from exploitation, abuse and neglect. Key issues focus on the socially constructed nature of child abuse and neglect, the multiple discourses associated with public health, the extent of state intervention in the lives of children and their families and the many contextual challenges facing nurses, midwives and health visitors. The invisibility of much safeguarding work is also discussed as we argue for greater understanding and recognition of the nursing contribution to child protection by other professional groups. Finally the chapter identifies that further research is needed to increase understanding about the nursing contribution to safeguarding work and the protection of children and young people.

The chapters in this book have all discussed nursing (in its many different guises), public health and child protection. They have examined a range of issues including the key elements of a public health approach to child maltreatment and the important role that nurses have in prevention and early identification work with children, young people and their families.

We now describe some of the challenges and opportunities arising from examining child protection and nursing through a public health lens. We consider how our changing understandings of child abuse and neglect and an increasing evidence base about this topic impacts upon policy and nursing practice. We highlight some critical debates about public health itself and consider the implications of this for preventative nursing work too. We also draw attention to the challenges facing nurses, midwives and health visitors in undertaking child protection work; these are numerous and include recognising and responding to new knowledge, shifting political landscapes, new policy and complex work environments where 'the demands of bureaucracy' abound (Munro, 2011, p. 6) as well as near continual organisational change.

This chapter contextualises nursing work in this area within wider multidisciplinary contexts, arguing for greater understanding and recognition by other professional groups of nursing's involvement in child protection. Gaps in the evidence base and the need for further research to inform policy and practice about nurses' work in protecting children and young people are highlighted. The chapter concludes with some final reflections on ongoing policy developments and the expanding knowledge base on child maltreatment, public health and nursing.

Child Protection, Public Health and Nursing: Opportunities and Challenges

Contributors to this book have described an increased understanding about the potential vulnerability to harm of children and young people at various stages over the life course. These range from babies living with parental substance misuse and/or domestic violence (Brandon *et al.*, 2010; Manning, 2011; Cuthbert *et al.*, 2011) to teenagers at risk of sexual perpetrators via the internet and social media (Balfe *et al.*, 2014). Indeed evidence about the extent, impact and costs of child maltreatment outlined in Chapter 2 provides a very clear rationale for adopting a public health approach to address the problem. Nonetheless adopting public health approaches to tackle the problem of child maltreatment is not without challenges (Peckover and Smith, 2011) – these are outlined below along with the implications for nurses.

Revisiting 'child maltreatment': New understandings and risks
One such challenge in adopting a public health approach to address child maltreatment lies with how the problem itself is understood. As outlined in the introductory chapter the concepts of 'child maltreatment', 'child abuse' and 'neglect' are socially constructed (Parton *et al.*, 1997; Parton, 2014); this means that what counts as child maltreatment or abuse shifts as societal norms and understandings change. This can be illustrated by child sexual abuse – an area of child maltreatment where our knowledge about the scale and range of the problem has altered as insight is gained both from victims' accounts (Berelowitz *et al.*, 2013; Melrose, 2013; CSJ, 2014) and evidence relating to recent and historical scandals about child sexual

abuse and exploitation (Brown *et al.*, 2011; Gray and Watt, 2013; Jay, 2014; Lampard and Marsden, 2015; Oxfordshire Safeguarding Children Board, 2015). Such changes in how child maltreatment is understood and the risks facing children and young people have implications for nurses; it often alters the focus of their work and creates new opportunities for practice (Peckover, 2009; 2013; Watson and Rodwell, 2014). This can be evidenced for example by the changing public health roles of SCPHNs, which have shifted to recognising the population level factors that are important in building resilience among children and their parents, identifying needs and risk early and delivering extra help and support where it is required (NHS England, 2014; PHE, 2014).

Other examples of where new risks and knowledge have translated into new and/or different practices for nurses includes midwives and health visitors delivering *Baby Steps*, an antenatal programme for mother and fathers which focuses upon the physical and emotional aspects of parenthood and the infant's well-being (Hogg *et al.*, 2015). Cole's work on preventing non-accidental head injury has been important in raising awareness of the importance of protecting babies' heads (Kemp and Coles, 2003; Coles, 2006; Coles and Collins, 2007; 2009). Another example, 'Think baby', is an online learning resource which has been developed to help student health visitors build their skills in observing and assessing mother–infant interactions (Appleton *et al.*, 2014), in recognition of the importance of sensitive and attuned parenting in promoting secure mother–infant attachments (Ranson and Urichuk, 2008; Murray, 2014). Meanwhile school nurses, with their growing awareness of the indicators of child sexual exploitation (DH, 2014c), are increasingly involved in identifying and working with young people who are vulnerable or victims of this type of abuse (DH and PHE, 2015). The invaluable contribution of school nurses here lies both in the universal and non-stigmatising nature of their role and that young people feel they can confide in them (Kirtley, 2013; Littler, 2014). Thus as our knowledge about risks to children and young people and what constitutes child maltreatment expands, this impacts upon the scope of public health nursing work; which not only creates role opportunities but also brings with it resource implications.

The focus upon parenting

Another challenge lies in how the solution to tackling child maltreatment through a public health approach is constructed. This is shaped in the policy and political arena, and, because the underlying causes of child maltreatment are highly complex, pragmatic and populist solutions are often adopted. Thus at the moment in the UK debates about the prevention of child maltreatment are largely framed in relation to parenting, with much interest in both universal and targeted measures to improve parenting (Gilbert *et al.*, 2012; Barlow and Calam, 2011; DH, 2014a). Again this has a number of implications for nurses.

It offers opportunities for public health nurses particularly midwives and health visitors to support parenting on a universal and early intervention basis. As detailed elsewhere in this book this is implicit within the HCP and underpinning evidence base (DH, 2009a; PHE, 2015) and is supported for example by the contribution that public health nurses make to delivering parenting programmes (see for example Parker and Kirk, 2006; Whittaker and Cowley, 2012; Kirkpatrick *et al.*, 2007; Byrne *et al.*, 2010). Moreover the Family Nurse Partnership, delivered by public health nurses, provides an important template for evidence-based primary prevention and early help parenting programmes (Barnes *et al.*, 2011; Ball *et al.*, 2012; MacMillan *et al.*, 2009). The current investment in health visiting outlined in Chapter 3 has probably also been shaped by these debates.

Neuroscientific evidence which links sensitive parenting and attachment to early brain development (see for example Schore, 2001; Nelson *et al.*, 2009; Parsons *et al.*, 2010) is also currently having an enormous impact on UK policy (Allen, 2011a; DH, 2009a; Macvarish *et al.*, 2014). In particular it has shaped the drive for early intervention to promote emotional well-being in the early years (Underdown and Barlow, 2012; Macvarish *et al.*, 2014; APPG, 2015). This reflects the life-course approach which is implicit within public health; as the WHO (2013, p. 3) has argued: 'What happens in childhood has a strong influence throughout the life-course.' The robust critical debate questioning how neuroscience has been translated into child and family policy is however worth noting (Bruer, 1999; Featherstone *et al.*, 2013; Wastell and White, 2012; Macvarish *et al.*, 2014; Edwards *et al.*, 2015). These authors suggest that, rather than being a good example of evidence-based policymaking, scientific claims have been inflated and used to justify prior policy ambitions. This illustrates again the contested and changing nature of knowledge in this area – which of course has implications for nursing.

The impact of austerity

One of the consequences of this current policy preoccupation with parenting and baby's brains – which are of course extremely pertinent issues of concern – is that it takes political and professional attention away from the wider social and economic context in which children, young people and families live (Marmot *et al.*, 2010; NCB, 2013). As Parton (2006; 2014) argues, the state plays a particular role in shaping child protection and how we respond to it. So it may be unsurprising that a Conservative-led Coalition government was pursuing policies concerned with parenting while at the same time reducing wider welfare services that supported children and families and improved their economic circumstances (Taylor-Gooby, 2012; Reed, 2012). Austerity measures such as reductions in the provision of benefits and services are adversely impacting upon child welfare as well as families and households more generally (Featherstone *et al.*, 2012; Reed, 2012; Scullin and Galloway, 2014; Women's Aid, 2015). This has important implications for nurses in their child protection role as it impacts upon their ability to deliver services themselves, access wider support and resources, and make referrals to and secure input from other services (Appleton, 2012). There are also concerns about the workforce capacity of nursing, particularly school nursing, across the UK (RCN, 2012), which has not seen the sustained investment as in health visiting (DH, 2011; Scottish Government, 2014a), and in many areas school nurses are struggling to fulfil role requirements.

Extrafamilial abuse

The focus upon parenting also firmly places child maltreatment within a familial context and moves attention away from extrafamilial abuse. This is indeed worrying given recent developments about the harms facing children and young people from extrafamilial contexts such as technology and social media, extrafamilial sexual abuse and child sexual exploitation (Dombrowski *et al.*, 2007; Jay, 2014; Balfe *et al.*, 2014). In particular the recent Jay report into child sexual exploitation in Rotherham (Jay, 2014) and Bedford's report in Oxfordshire (Oxfordshire Safeguarding Children Board, 2015) have provided a glimpse of the likely scale of the problem and provides further evidence of the value of adopting a public health approach underpinned by epidemiology. Clearly identifying patterns of concern within a population of vulnerable children and young people – and using this epidemiological knowledge constructively – could contribute to a strategic response to addressing this problem (Brown *et al.*, 2011).

Re-examining 'public health'

This book is primarily concerned with public health, but it is worth noting that public health is itself not without critiques. Sociologists have pointed towards the ways that public health is concerned with the surveillance and regulation of the population (see for example Lupton, 1995; Nettleton and Bunton, 1995; Petersen and Lupton, 1996). Examples abound in the literature but public health interventions focusing upon aspects of mothering and family life have been offered as key examples of this (see for example Murphy, 2003; Lupton, 2011; Wyness, 2012). Such critical debates about regulation, privacy and surveillance underpinning public health clearly have pertinence for nurses working in public health, particularly those concerned with child welfare and protection. Indeed a public health approach to child maltreatment expands 'state intervention' or 'interest' in children and families, and for public health nurses it expands their professional gaze (Peckover, 2009; 2013). Debates about the role of professionals undertaking state intervention in families are evident in relation to social work and health visiting (see for example Parton, 1991; Peckover, 2002; Marcellus, 2005; Kent *et al.*, 2011), but this is an area which could be further considered particularly in relation to the contribution of the wider nursing workforce.

As well as critical debates about its role, the concept of public health itself is not straightforward. This is because 'public health' incorporates different approaches often categorised as 'bio-medical' or 'community development' (Baggott, 2011). Moreover public health work and its knowledge base are multidisciplinary, draw upon a wide range of policy and practice frameworks and involve numerous activities and interventions. They also respond to wider societal and contextual issues, including government reforms and election cycles. Such diversity can make 'public health' work difficult to conceptualise fully; this may be a particular problem for those working in roles where public health work is not explicit: for example, nurses working in urgent and unscheduled care settings.

As the chapters in this book have outlined, nurses have an important role in prevention and early identification work with children, young people and their families through a public health approach. One of the key steps in adopting a public health approach to identifying child maltreatment is getting to the bottom of the size and extent of the problem (WHO, 2013). Data from the National Child and Maternal Health Intelligence Network and the Public Health Outcomes Framework developed by the Department of Health provide evidence about the wider determinants of ill health, but there is a scarcity of data around child abuse and neglect. For example, Action for Children has highlighted that most local authorities do not know the scale of child neglect in their areas (Burgess *et al.*, 2012; 2014). Public health nurses and particularly those in leadership and managerial roles should be influencing local authorities to gather relevant data which accurately reflects the extent of the problem.

Making 'nursing' visible?
It is also important to appreciate that the nursing contribution to addressing child maltreatment takes place within a wider multi-agency context; indeed collaborative work is central to both public health activity and safeguarding work (HM Government, 2015). However the nursing, midwifery and health visiting input to safeguarding children may not always be clearly recognised or indeed conceptualised as such by those undertaking preventative work with children and families (see Peckover, 2013; Kent *et al.*, 2011). Thus there is an urgency for these roles – and in particular nurses' involvement in addressing child maltreatment – to be more clearly

articulated. In doing so it is important to adopt not only a realistic view of the nursing contribution to the prevention of child maltreatment and child protection but also to think creatively about what is being achieved. This may involve recognising and delineating the small maybe mundane aspects of nursing work which nevertheless serve to prevent problems occurring, to promote resilience or to protect children. Often small acts involving anticipatory guidance, prevention or early detection can make a big difference, and nurses can do this well. What is required however is an increased visibility of these elements of the nursing role and how it relates to safeguarding children.

The complexities associated with this work – particularly in relation to relationships with clients and decision-making – have been well illustrated in Chapter 6, which focuses upon early detection. It is also evident in Chapter 3, which has outlined health visiting practice within the new English service model of health visiting (DH, 2014a) including some of the preventative approaches which can help to build parents' coping and resilience skills, as well as modify risky situations.

In considering the nursing contribution to protecting children it is also important to acknowledge differences across the workforce, in relation to skills, practices, contexts and opportunities to work with children and families. The pivotal role that nurses can play in a range of practice settings has been illustrated in Chapter 5, which emphasises that safeguarding is 'everyone's responsibility' (HM Government, 2015, p. 9), reflecting a whole systems approach and is illustrated through examples of children's and young people's healthcare journeys. Importantly this chapter draws attention to the RCPCH's 'intercollegiate document', which details the knowledge, skills and competencies required by all nurses and midwives to ensure effective safeguarding and child protection practice (RCPCH, 2014).

The location and prominence of leadership in safeguarding work in acute care organisations is also an area where greater attention is required, in terms of the visibility of safeguarding as part of the wider quality and patient safety agendas and the important requirement for safeguarding leads to remain clinically

connected. This is an area that has received limited previous attention. Chapter 7 examined some of the important challenges for
nurse leaders and designated post holders when safeguarding lead
roles sit within an acute NHS provider organisation.

Even though *Child Protection, Public Health and Nursing* focuses
largely on the UK context where there is a particularly well-developed child protection system and public health nursing workforce
(Gilbert *et al.*, 2011), the issues may be different elsewhere. Thus
the need for international comparative research as discussed in
Chapter 4 is useful. In undertaking such an analysis, an appreciation of the role of nurses in relation to the wider political and
policy context in which they work is required. This includes but
also goes beyond formal child protection systems. So while in an
international context general debates may be similar, their appli-
cation or operationalisation in different contexts are likely to vary.

Future Research
A central tenet of public health is prevention and early intervention,
yet this requires evidence of effectiveness of interventions (WHO,
2013). Here is a dilemma, as there are of course many challenges
in proving the effectiveness of something that prevents something
happening. So judging 'what works?' is a key tension in public
health, and due to the nature and antecedents of child maltreatment
it is particularly problematic to provide evidence for the effectiveness of prevention and early intervention activities to address child
abuse and neglect (Gilbert *et al.*, 2012; WHO, 2013).

Indeed interestingly, while the important role played by health
services in preventing child maltreatment is acknowledged, much
of the discussion about this in the recent academic/public health
literature has been focused upon the role of doctors, notably GPs
and paediatricians, or the 'primary care team' (see Gilbert *et al.*,
2012; Woodman *et al.*, 2014). While acknowledging these groups
have an important role, this book has been about the role of
nurses, and it fills an important gap in the literature. However as
many of its contributors have highlighted there is limited research
about nurses in relation to child protection and maltreatment.
The need for further research around public health roles, nursing

practices and how these influence child outcomes are important imperatives for the future.

Much nursing work around early intervention and prevention also remains invisible, in terms of both a robust evidence base and a paucity of relevant literature to articulate the range of nursing roles. In terms of future research, there is a need to build on the priorities identified in *From Evidence Into Action* (PHE, 2014) and the updated evidence for the HCP (PHE, 2015) to demonstrate the impact of nursing work. There need to be creative ways of capturing and measuring the long-term impact and contribution of nursing in the prevention of child abuse and neglect and in the protection of children and young people. A more robust academic debate about the roles and contribution of nurses to safeguarding children – and the challenges and opportunities this brings – would also be welcomed.

Conclusions

Establishing effectiveness is important for securing resources for preventative work; this may occur now more easily for illness prevention strategies but there are a number of further steps to be taken before the problem of child abuse and neglect is fully embedded as a public health priority. Securing investment for preventative work is always difficult, but more so in an era of fiscal austerity and public sector funding cuts. Achieving this requires a shift in resources, services and orientation – and requires a long-term view both in relation to politics and policy, and also through the media. In the UK in particular, child deaths and serious incidents have driven much child protection policy, and the adoption of a public health approach requires a societal and media shift from a reactive to proactive point of view, supported by difficult resource decisions. As Gilbert *et al.* (2012, p. 327) point out: 'A preventive approach to child maltreatment is slowly gaining momentum, but effective translation into practice has been patchy.'

As frontline healthcare professionals, nurses, midwives and health visitors have a key role to play in this agenda through their work with children and young people. Nurses as part of the wider children's workforce continually work amidst policy reforms, organisational change, government reorganisations and election cycles, so alongside their safeguarding children work there is a theme of continual change and flux. Integrated working within health and local authority arrangements to improve the planning, delivery and review of services for children, young people and their families is a key current issue. It is time for nursing to acknowledge its important role, mobilise the profession and be more proactive in all aspects of safeguarding children research, policy and practice.

Summary

Child Protection, Public Health and Nursing has brought together a series of chapters which explore the important contribution of the nursing workforce in the prevention of child maltreatment and in the protection of children and young people. This chapter has synthesised the key themes emerging from the previous chapters and the many opportunities and challenges facing the nursing workforce, including a brief re-examination of public health, the current policy focus and interest in parenting, issues concerning extrafamilial abuse, the impact of austerity on services and practice and the need to make 'nursing' practice more visible in this crucial area of work. Areas for future research are highlighted and include in particular a need for greater examination of nurses' roles in prevention and early identification work with children, young people and their families.

REFERENCES

Adams, C. (2012) 'The history of health visiting', *Nursing in Practice*. Vol. 68. Available from URL: http://www.nursinginpractice.com/article/history-health-visiting

Ahmad, F., Driver, N., McNally, M. J. and Stewart, D. E. (2009) ' "Why doesn't she seek help for partner abuse?" An exploratory study with South Asian immigrant women', *Social Science & Medicine*, Vol. 69, No. 4, pp. 613–22

Alexander, H., Macdonald, E. and Paton, S. (2005) 'Raising the issue of domestic abuse in school', *Children and Society*, Vol. 19, No. 3, pp.187–98

All Wales Child Protection Procedures Review Group (2008) 'All Wales child protection procedures' (online). Available from URL: www.awcpp.org.uk/wp-content/uploads/2014/03/All-Wales-Child-Protection-Procedures-2008.pdf (accessed 13 February 2015)

Allen, G. (2011a) *Early Intervention: The Next Steps*, an independent report to HM Government, London: Cabinet Office. Available from URL: www.gov.uk/government/uploads/system/uploads/attachment_data/file/284086/early-intervention-next-steps2.pdf (accessed 15 June 2015)

Allen, G. (2011b) *Early Intervention: Smart Investment, Massive Savings*, the second independent report to HM Government, London: Cabinet Office. Available from URL : www.gov.uk/government/uploads/system/uploads/attachment_data/file/61012/earlyintervention-smartinvestment.pdf (accessed 15 June 2015)

APPG (2015) *Building Great Britons. Conception To Age 2: First 1,001 Days*, London: All Party Parliamentary Group and WAVE Trust. Available from URL: www.1001criticaldays.co.uk/news_detail.php?id=73 (accessed 30 March 2015)

Appleton, J. V. (1994) 'The role of the health visitor in identifying and working with vulnerable families in relation to child protection: A review of the literature', *Journal of Advanced Nursing*, Vol. 20, pp. 167–75

Appleton, J. V. (1996) 'Working with vulnerable families: A health visiting perspective', *Journal of Advanced Nursing*, Vol. 23, No. 5, pp. 912–18

Appleton, J. V. (2011) 'Safeguarding and protecting children: Where is health visiting now?', *Community Practitioner*, Vol. 84, No. 11, pp. 21–5

Appleton, J. V. (2012) 'Delivering safeguarding children services in primary care – Responding to national child protection policy', *Primary Health Care: Research and Development*, Vol. 13, No. 1, pp. 60–71

Appleton, J. V. (in press) 'Vulnerable school aged children', in Debell, D. (in press) *Public Health for Children* (2nd edn), London: Hodder

Appleton, J. V. and Cowley, S. (2004) 'The guideline contradiction – Health visitors' use of formal guidelines for identifying and assessing families in need', *International Journal of Nursing Studies*, Vol. 41, pp. 785–97

Appleton, J. V. and Clemerson-Trew, J. (2008) 'Safeguarding children', in Cowley, S. (ed.) (2008) *Public Health in Policy and Practice. A Sourcebook for Health Visitors* (2nd edn), London: Baillière Tindall, pp. 258–83

Appleton, J. V. and Cowley, S. (2008a) 'Health visiting assessment processes under scrutiny: A case study of knowledge use during family health needs assessments', *International Journal of Nursing Studies*, Vol. 45, No. 5, pp. 682–96

Appleton, J. V. and Cowley, S. (2008b) 'Health visiting assessment principles – Unpacking critical attributes in health visitor needs assessment practice: A case study', *International Journal of Nursing Studies*, Vol. 45, No. 2, pp. 232–45

Appleton, J. V., Harris, M., Kelly, C. and Huppe, I. (2014) ' "Think baby": Online learning for student health visitors', *Community Practitioner*, Vol. 87, No. 6, pp. 20–3

Audit Commission (2010), 'Giving children a healthy start' (online). Available from URL: http://archive.audit-commission.gov.uk/auditcommission/SiteCollectionDocuments/Downloads/201002-GivingChildrenHealth-Start_report_WEB.pdf (accessed 5 January 2015)

Bacchus, L., Mezey, G. and Bewley, S. (2002) 'Women's perceptions and experiences of routine enquiry for domestic violence in a maternity service', *BJOG: An International Journal of Obstetrics and Gynaecology*, Vol. 109, No. 1, pp. 9–16

Baggott, R. (2011) *Public Health, Policy and Politics*, 2nd edn, Basingstoke: Palgrave Macmillan

Balfe, M., Gallagher, B., Masson, H., Balfe, S., Brugha, R. and Hackett, S. (2014). 'Internet child sex offenders' concerns about online security and their use of identity protection technologies: A review', *Child Abuse Review* (online); doi:10.1002/car.2308

Ball, M., Barnes, J. and Meadows, P. (2012) *Issues Emerging from the First 10 Pilot Sites Implementing the Nurse-Family Partnership Home-Visiting Programme in England*, London, Department of Health

Balmer, R., Gibson, E. and Harris, J. (2010) 'Understanding child neglect: Current perspectives in dentistry', *Primary Dental Care*, Vol. 17, No. 3, pp. 105–9

Barker, K. (2014) *A New Settlement for Health and Social Care: Final Report*, London: King's Fund

Barlow, J. and Calam, R. (2011) 'A public health approach to safeguarding in the 21st century', *Child Abuse Review*, Vol. 20, No. 4, pp. 238–55

Barlow, J., Davis, H., McIntosh, E., Jarrett, P., Mockford, C. and Stewart-Brown, S. (2007). 'Role of home visiting in improving parenting and health in families at risk of abuse and neglect: Results of a multicentre randomised controlled trial and economic evaluation', *Archives of Disease in Childhood*, Vol. 92, No. 3, pp. 229–33

Barlow, J., Fisher, J. D. and Jones, D. (2012) *Systematic Review of Models of*

Analysing Significant Harm. Research Report DFE–RR199, London: Department for Education

Barnes, J., Ball, M., Medows, P., Howden, B., Jackson, A., Henderson, J. and Niven, L. (2011) *The Family-Nurse Partnership Programme in England and Wales: Wave 1 Implementation in Toddlerhood and a Comparison Between Waves 1 and 2a Implementation in Pregnancy and Infancy*, London: Department of Health

Berelowitz, S., Clifton, J., Firmin, C., Gulyurtlu, S. and Edwards, G. (2013) *If Only Someone Had Listened*, Office of the Children's Commissioner's Enquiry into Child Sexual Exploitation in Gangs and Groups Final Report, London: Office of the Children's Commissioner

Beynon, C. E., Gutmanis, I. A., Tutty, L. M., Wathen, C. N. and Mac-Millan, H. L. (2012) 'Why physicians and nurses ask (or don't) about partner violence. A qualitative analysis', *BMC Public Health*; doi:10.1186/1471–2458–12–473

Blair, M., Stewart-Brown, S., Waterston, T. and Crowther, R. (2010) *Child Public Health,* Oxford: Oxford University Press

Bloor, M. and McIntosh, J. (1990) 'Surveillance and concealment: A comparison of techniques of client resistance in therapeutic communities and health visiting', in Cunningham-Burley, S. and McKegany, N. (eds) (1990) *Readings in Medical Sociology*, London: Tavistock, pp. 159–81

Bradbury-Jones, C. (2009) 'Globalisation and its implications for health care and nursing practice', *Nursing Standard,* Vol. 23, No. 25, pp. 3–47

Bradbury-Jones, C. (2013) 'Refocusing child protection supervision: An innovative approach to supporting practitioners', *Child Care in Practice*, Vol. 19, No. 3, pp. 253–66

Bradbury-Jones, C., Innes, N., Evans, D., Ballantyne, F. and Taylor, J. (2013) 'Dental neglect as a marker of broader neglect: A qualitative investigation of public health nurses assessments of oral health in preschool children', *BMC Public Health*, Vol. 13, p. 370; doi:10.1186/1471–2458–13–370

Bradbury-Jones, C., Taylor, J., Kroll, T. and Duncan, F. (2014) 'Domestic abuse awareness and recognition among primary healthcare professionals and abused women: A qualitative investigation', *Journal of Clinical Nursing*; doi:10.1111/jocn.12534

Brandon, M., Bailey, S., Belderson, P., Warren, C., Howe, D., Gardner, R., Sidebotham, P., Dodsworth, J. and Black, J. (2008) *Analysing Child Deaths and Serious Injuries through Abuse and Neglect: What Can We Learn? A Biennial Analysis of Serious Case Reviews 2003–2005*, London: Department for Children, Schools and Families

Brandon, M., Bailey, S., Belderson, P., Gardner, R., Sidebotham, P., Dodsworth, J., Warren, C. and Black, J. (2009) *Understanding Serious Case Reviews and Their Impact: A Biennial Analysis of Serious Case Reviews 2005–2007*, London: Department for Children, Schools and Families

Brandon, M, Bailey, S. and Belderson, P. (2010) *Building on the Learning from Serious Case Reviews: A Two-Year Analysis of Child Protection Database Notifications 2007–2009*, London: Department for Education. Available from URL: www.gov.uk/government/uploads/system/uploads/

attachment_data/file/181651/DFE-RR040.pdf (accessed 4 January 2015)

Brandon, M., Sidebotham, P., Bailey, S., Belderson, P., Hawley, C., Ellis, C. and Megson, M. (2012) *New Learning from Serious Case Reviews: A Two Year Report for 2009–2011*, London: Department for Education

Brandon, M., Bailey, S., Belderson, P. and Larsson, B. (2013) 'Neglect and serious case reviews: A report from the University of East Anglia commissioned by the NSPCC' (online). Available from URL: www.nspcc.org.uk/globalassets/documents/research-reports/neglect-serious-case-reviews-report.pdf (accessed 5 January 2015).

Bronfenbrenner, U. (1979) *The Ecology of Human Development*, Cambridge. MA: Harvard University Press

Brown, A. (2012) 'Preventing drug and alcohol use by school children', *Community Practitioner*, Vol. 85, No. 2, pp. 38–42

Brown, D. W., Anda, R. F., Tiemeier, H., Felitti, V. J., Edwards, V. J., Croft, J. B., Giles, W. H. (2009) 'Adverse childhood experiences and the risk of premature mortality', *American Journal of Preventive Medicine*, Vol. 37, No. 5, pp. 389–96

Brown, J., O'Donnell, T. and Erooga, M. (2011) *Sexual Abuse: A Public Health Challenge*, London: NSPCC. Available from URL: www.nspcc.org.uk/globalassets/documents/research-reports/sexual-abuse--public-health-challenge-evidence-review.pdf (accessed 5 January 2015)

Brown, R. and Ward, H. (2013) *Decision-Making Within a Child's Timeframe. An Overview of Current Research Evidence for Family Justice Professionals Concerning Child Development and the Impact of Child Maltreatment: Working Paper 16*, London: Childhood Wellbeing Research Centre

Browne, K. (1995) 'Preventing child maltreatment through community nursing', *Journal of Advanced Nursing*, Vol. 21, No. 1, pp. 57–63

Browne, K. D. and Saqi, S. (1988) 'Approaches to screening families at high risk for child abuse', in Browne, K. D., Davies, C. and Stratton, P. (eds) (1998) *Early Prediction and Prevention of Child Abuse*, Chichester: Wiley, pp. 57–85

Bruer, J. T. (1999) *The Myth of the First Three Years*, New York, NY: The Free Press

Buck, L. and Collins, S. (2007) 'Why don't midwives ask about domestic abuse?', *British Journal of Midwifery*, Vol. 15, No. 12, pp. 753–8

Burgess, C., Daniel, B., Scott, J., Mulley, K., Derbyshire, D. and Downie, M. (2012) *Child Neglect in 2011*, an annual review by Action for Children in partnership with the University of Stirling, London: Action for Children. Available from URL: www.actionforchildren.org.uk/ (accessed 30 March 2015)

Burgess, C., Daniel, B., Scott, J., Dobbin, H., Mulley, K. and Whitfield E. (2014). *Preventing Child Neglect in the UK: What Makes Services Accessible to Children and Families?*, an annual review by Action for Children in partnership with the University of Stirling, Watford: Action for Children. Available from URL: www.actionforchildren.org.uk (accessed 30 March 2015)

Byrne, E., Holland, S. and Jerzembek, G. (2010). 'A pilot study on the impact of a home-based parenting intervention: Parents plus', *Child Care in Practice,* Vol. 16, No. 2, pp. 111–27

CAADA (2014) *In Plain Sight: Affective Help for Children Exposed to Domestic Abuse,* Bristol: Co-ordinated Action against Domestic Abuse

Cawson, P., Wattam, C., Brooker, S. and Kelly, G. (2000) *Child Maltreatment in the United Kingdom: A Study of the Prevalence of Abuse and Neglect,* London: NSPCC

Chief Secretary to the Treasury (2003) *Every Child Matters,* cmnd 5860, London: The Stationery Office

Children Act (1989). Available from URL: www.legislation.gov.uk/ ukpga/1989/41/contents (accessed 13 February 2015)

Children Act (2004). Available from URL: www.legislation.gov.uk/ ukpga/2004/31/contents (accessed 13 February 2015)

Children (Northern Ireland) Order (1995). Available from URL: www.legislation.gov.uk/nisi/1995/755/contents (accessed 13 February 2015)

Children (Scotland) Act (1995). Available from URL: www.legislation.gov.uk/ ukpga/1995/36/contents (accessed 13 February 2015)

Children's Rights Director (2004) *Safe From Harm: Children's Views Report,* London: Commission for Social Care Inspection

Clarke, M. L. (2000) 'Out of the wilderness and into the fold: The school nurse and child protection', *Child Abuse Review,* Vol. 9, No. 5. pp. 364–74

Coles, L. (2006) *Protecting Babies' Heads: A Teaching Tool Box for Preventing Shaking and Head Injuries in Babies,* London: Community Practitioners and Health Visitors Association

Coles, L. and Collins, L. (2007) 'Barriers to and facilitators for preventing shaking and head injuries in babies', *Community Practitioner,* Vol. 80, No. 10, pp. 20–4

Coles, L. and Collins, L. (2009) 'Including fathers in preventing non-accidental head injury', *Community Practitioner,* Vol. 82, No. 4, pp. 20–3

Community Practitioners' and Health Visitors' Association (CPHVA) (2007) The Distinctive Contribution of Health Visiting to Public Health and Well-being. Addressing public health priorities using the Principles of Health Visiting. London: Unite/CPHVA Health Visiting Forum.

Corby, B., Shemmings, D. and Wilkins, D. (2012) *Child Abuse: An Evidence Base For Confident Practice* (4th edn), Maidenhead: The Open University Press/McGraw-Hill Education

Corso, P. S., Edwards, V. J., Fang, X. and Mercy, J. A. (2008) 'Health-related quality of life among adults who experienced maltreatment during childhood', *American Journal of Public Health,* Vol. 98, No. 6, pp.1094–100

Cowley, S. (1995) 'In health visiting, the routine visit is one that has passed', *Journal of Advanced Nursing,* Vol. 22, No. 2, pp. 276–84

Cowley, S. (2008) *Public Health in Policy and Practice: A Sourcebook for Health Visitors and Community Nurses,* Edinburgh: Baillière Tindall Elsevier

Cowley, S. and Appleton, J.V. (2000) 'The Search for Health Needs', in Appleton, J.V. and Cowley, S. (eds.) *The Search for Health Needs. Research for Health Visiting Practice,* Basingstoke, Macmillan Press Ltd, pp.1-24.

Cowley, S. and Frost, M. (2006) *The Principles of Health Visiting: Opening the*

Doors to Public Health Practice in the 21st Century, London: Amicus

Cowley, S. and Houston, A. M. (2003) 'A structured health needs assessment tool: Acceptability and effectiveness for health visiting', *Journal of Advanced Nursing,* Vol. 43, No. 1, pp. 82–92

Cowley, S., Caan, W., Dowling, S. and Weir, H. (2007) 'What do health visitors do? A "state" of activities and service organisation', *Public Health,* Vol. 121, pp. 869–79

Cowley, S., Kemp, L., Day, C. and Appleton, J. V. (2012) 'Research and the organization of complex provision: Conceptualising health visiting services and early years programmes', *Journal of Research in Nursing,* Vol. 17, No. 2, pp. 108–24

Cowley, S., Whittaker, K., Grigulis, A., Malone, M., Donetto, S., Wood, H., Morrow, E. and Maben, J. (2013) 'Why health visiting? A review of the literature about key health visitor interventions, processes and outcomes for children and families' (online), Available from URL: www.kcl.ac.uk/nursing/research/nnru/publications/Reports/Why-Health-Visiting-NNRU-report-12-02-2013.pdf (accessed 13 July 2015)

Cowley, S., Whittaker, K., Malone, M., Donetto, S., Grigulis, A. and Maben, J. (2014) 'Why health visiting? Examining the potential public health benefits from health visiting practice within a universal service: A narrative review of the literature', *International Journal of Nursing Studies,* Vol. 52, No. 1, pp. 465–80

Crisp, B. R. and Lister, P. G. (2004) 'Child protection and public health: Nurses' responsibilities', *Journal of Advanced Nursing,* Vol. 47, No. 6, pp. 656–63

CSJ (2014) *Girls and Gangs. XLP,* London: The Centre for Social Justice

Cuthbert, C., Rayns, G. and Stanley, K. (2011) *All Babies Count: Prevention and Protection for Vulnerable Babies,* London: NSPCC

Daniel, B. (2015) 'Why have we made neglect so complicated? Taking a fresh look at noticing and helping the neglected child', *Child Abuse Review,* Vol. 24, No. 2, pp. 82–94; doi:10.1002/car.2296

Daniel, B., Taylor, J. S. and Scott, J. (2011) *Recognizing and Helping the Neglected Child: Evidence-Based Practice for Assessment and Intervention,* London: Jessica Kingsley

Davies, C. and Ward, H. (2012) *Safeguarding Children Across Services: Messages from Research,* London: Jessica Kingsley

Day, P. (2005) '"Coping with our kids": A pilot evaluation of a parenting programme delivered by school nurses', *Groupwork,* Vol. 15, No. 1, pp. 42–60

De Bell, D. (2007). *Public Health Practice and the School-Age Population.* London: Hodder-Arnold

DH (1995) *Child Protection: Messages from Research,* London: HMSO

DH (2000) *No Secrets: Guidance on Developing and Implementing Multi-Agency Policies and Procedures to Protect Vulnerable Adults from Abuse,* London: The Stationery Office

DH (2004) *Practice Based Commissioning: Promoting Clinical Engagement,* London: Department of Health

DH (2008) *High Quality Care for All: NHS Next Stage Review Final Report,*

London: The Stationery Office

DH (2009a) *Healthy Child Programme: Pregnancy and the First Five Years of Life*, London: Department of Health. Available from URL: www.gov.uk/government/publications/healthy-child-programme-pregnancy-and-the-first-5-years-of-life (accessed 5 January 2015)

DH (2009b) *Healthy Child Programme from 5–19 Years Old*, London: The Stationery Office

DH (2010) *Healthy Lives, Healthy People*, London: The Stationery Office

DH (2011) *Health Visitor Implementation Plan 2011–15: A Call to Action February 2011*, London: Department of Health. Available from URL: www.gov.uk/government/uploads/system/uploads/attachment_data/file/213110/Health-visitor-implementation-plan.pdf (accessed 15 June 2015)

DH (2013a) *Our Children Deserve Better: Prevention Pays*, annual report of the chief medical officer 2012, London: Department of Health

DH (2013b) *The National Health Visitor Plan: Progress to Date and Implementation 2013 Onwards*, London: Department of Health

DH (2014a) *Overview 1: National Health Visiting Programme*, London: Department of Health

DH (2014b) *Overview of the Six Early Years High Impact Areas.* London: Department of Health. Available from URL: www.gov.uk/government/publications/commissioning-of-public-health-services-for-children (accessed 13 July 2015)

DH (2014c) *Health Working Group Report on Child Sexual Exploitation: Improving the Outcomes for Children by Promoting Effective Engagement of Health Services and Staff*, London: The Stationery Office

DH (2015) *4-5-6 Model.* London: Department of Health. Available from URL: https://vivbennett.blog.gov.uk/2015/03/05/the-4-5-6-model (accessed 13 July 2015)

DH Action on Health Visiting Programme and CPHVA (2009) *Getting It Right for Children and Families. Maximising the Contribution of the Health Visiting Team. 'Ambition, Action, Achievement'.* London: Department of Health

DH and PHE (2014) *A Framework for Personalised Care and Population Health for Nurses, Midwives, Health Visitors and Allied Health Professionals: Caring for Populations Across the Life-Course*, London: Public Health England

DH and PHE (2015) *School Nurse Programme: Supporting the Implementation of the New Service Offer: Helping School Nurses to Tackle Child Sexual Exploitation*, London: Department of Health

DHSSPS (2003) *Cooperating to Safeguard Children*, Belfast: Department of Health, Social Services and Public Safety

Dixon, L., Browne, K. and Hamilton-Giachritsis, C. (2009) 'Patterns of risk and protective factors in the intergenerational cycle of maltreatment', *Journal of Family Violence*, Vol. 24, No. 2, pp. 111–22

Dombrowski, S. C., Gischlar, K. L. and Durst, T. (2007), 'Safeguarding young people from cyber pornography and cyber sexual predation: A major dilemma of the internet', *Child Abuse Review*, Vol. 16, No. 3, pp. 153–70; doi:10.1002/car.939

Donetto, S., Malone, M., Hughes, J., Morrow, E., Cowley, S. and Maben, J. (2013) *Health Visiting: The Voice of Service Users. Learning From Service Users' Experiences to Inform the Development of UK Health Visiting Practice and Services*, London: King's College

Douglas, J. (2010) 'The rise of multi-disciplinary public health', in Douglas, J., Earle, S., Handsley S., Jones, L., Lloyd, C. E. and Spurr, S. (eds) (2010) *A Reader in Promoting Public Health: Challenge and Controversy*, Milton Keynes: Open University, pp. 9–14

Eastman, A. (2014) 'Enough is enough. A report on child protection and mental health services for children and young people' (online). Available from URL: www.centreforsocialjustice.org.uk/UserStorage/pdf/Pdf%20 reports/enough.pdf (accessed 5 January 2015)

ECI (2014) 'European competence initiative – Early childhood intervention' (online). Available from URL: www.early-intervention.eu (accessed 30 September 2014)

Edwards, R., Gillies, V. and Horsley, N. (2015) 'Early intervention and evidence-based policy and practice: Framing and taming', *Social Policy and Society*; doi:10.1017/S1474746415000081

Elkan, R., Kendrick, D., Hewitt, M., Robinson, J., Tolley, K., Blair, M., Dewey, M., Williams, D. and Brummel, K. (2000) 'The effectiveness of domiciliary visiting: A systematic review of international studies and a selective review of the British literature', *Health Technology Assessment*, Vol. 4, No. 13, pp. i–v, 1–339

Europa.eu (2014) 'The Schengen area and cooperation' (online). Available from URL: http://europa.eu/legislation_summaries/justice_freedom_security/free_movement_of_persons_asylum_immigration/l33020_en.htm (accessed 15 April 2014)

European Agency for Development in Special Needs Education (2005) *The Early Childhood Intervention Study*, Brussels: European Agency for Development

Faculty of Public Health (2010a) 'What is public health?' (online). Available from URL: www.fph.org.uk/what_is_public_health (accessed 12 August 2014)

Faculty of Public Health (2010b) 'Professional standards' (online). Available from URL: www.fph.org.uk/professional_standards (accessed 12 August 2014)

Fang, X., Brown, D., Florence, C. and Mercy, J. (2012) 'The economic burden of child maltreatment in the United States and implications for prevention', *Child Abuse & Neglect*, Vol. 36, No. 2, pp. 156–65

Fazel, M., Reed, R. V., Panter-Brick, C. and Stein, A. (2012) 'Mental health of displaced and refugee children resettled in high-income countries: Risk and protective factors', *The Lancet*, Vol. 379, No. 9812, pp. 266–82

Featherstone, B., Broadhurst, K. and Holt, K. (2012) 'Thinking systemically – thinking politically: Building strong partnerships with children and families in the context of rising inequality', *British Journal of Social Work*, Vol. 42, No. 4, pp. 618–33; doi:10.1093/bjsw/bcr080

Featherstone, B., Morris, K. and White, S. (2013) 'A marriage made in hell:

Early intervention meets child protection', *British Journal of Social Work*, Vol. 44, No. 7, pp. 1735–49; doi:10.1093/bjsw/bct052

Feder, G., Hutson, M., Ramsay, J. and Taket, A. (2006) 'Women exposed to intimate partner violence: Expectations and experiences when they encounter health care professionals: A meta-analysis of qualitative studies', *Archives of Internal Medicine*, Vol. 166, No. 1, pp. 22–37

Feder, G., Ramsay, J., Dunne, D., Rose, M., Arsene, C., Norman, R., Kuntze, S., Spencer, A., Bacchus, L., Hague, G., Warburton, A. and Taket, A. (2009) 'How far does screening women for domestic (partner) violence in different health-care settings meet criteria for a screening programme? Systematic reviews of nine UK National Screening Committee criteria', *Health Technology Assessment*, Vol. 13, No. 16, pp. 1–136

Felitti, V. J., Anda, R. F., Nordenberg, D., Williamson, D. F., Spitz, A. M., Edwards, V., Koss, M. P. and Marks, J. S. (1998) 'Relationship of childhood abuse and household dysfunction to many of the leading causes of death in adults. The Adverse Childhood Experiences (ACE) Study', *American Journal of Preventive Medicine*, Vol. 14, No. 4, pp. 245–58

Field, F. (2010) *The Foundation Years: Preventing Poor Children Becoming Poor Adults. The Report for the Independent Review on Poverty and Life Chances*, London: Cabinet Office

Flaherty, E. G., Sege, R. D., Griffith, J., Price, L. L., Wasserman, R., Slora, E., Dhepyasuwan, N., Harris, D., Norton, D., Angelilli, M. L., Abney, D. and Binns, H. J. (2008) 'From suspicion of physical child abuse to reporting: Primary care clinician decision-making', *Pediatrics*, Vol. 122, No. 3, pp. 611–19

Flynn, M. (2012) *Winterbourne View Hospital: A Serious Case Review*, South Gloucestershire: South Gloucestershire Safeguarding Adults Board

Flynn, R. (2002) 'Clinical governance and governmentality', *Health, Risk & Society*, Vol. 4, No. 2, pp. 155–73

Francis, R. (2013) *The Mid Staffordshire NHS Foundation Trust Public Inquiry*, London: Department of Health

Freymond, N. and Cameron, G. (eds) (2006) *Towards Positive Systems of Child and Family Welfare: International Comparisons of Child Protection*, Toronto: University of Toronto Press

Frost, M. (1999) 'Health visitors' perceptions of domestic violence: The private nature of the problem', *Journal of Advanced Nursing*, Vol. 30, No. 3, pp. 589–96

Gilbert, R., Kemp, A., Thoburn, J., Sidebotham, P., Radford, L., Glaser, D. and MacMillan, H. (2008) 'Recognising and responding to child maltreatment', *The Lancet*, Vol. 373, No. 9671, pp. 1250–1

Gilbert, R., Widom, C., Browne, K., Fergusson, D., Webb, E. and Janson, S. (2009a) 'Burden and consequences of child maltreatment in high-income countries', *The Lancet*, Vol. 373, No. 9657, pp. 68–81; doi:10.1016/S0140–6736(08)61706–7

Gilbert, R., Kemp, A., Thoburn, J., Sidebotham, P., Radford, L., Glaser, D. and MacMillan, H. (2009b) 'Recognising and responding to child maltreatment', *The Lancet*, Vol. 373, No. 9658, pp. 167–80

Gilbert, N., Parton, N. and Skivenes, M. (eds) (2011) *Child Protection Systems: International Trends and Orientations*, Oxford: Oxford University Press

Gilbert, R., Woodman, J. and Logan, S. (2012) 'Developing services for a public health approach to child maltreatment', *International Journal of Children's Rights*, Vol. 20, No. 3, pp. 323–42

Gillingham, P. (2011) 'Decision-making tools and the development of expertise in child protection practitioners: Are we "just breeding workers who are good at ticking boxes"?', *Child and Family Social Work*, Vol. 16, No. 4, pp. 412–21

Gove, M. (2010), letter from Michael Gove to Eileen Munro, 10 June 2010, London: Department for Education

Graham, H. (ed.) (2009) *Understanding Health Inequalities*, Maidenhead: Open University Press

Gray, D. and Watt, P. (2013) *Giving Victims a Voice. Joint Report on Sexual Allegations Made Against Jimmy Savile*, London: Metropolitan Police Service and NSPCC

Hackett, A. J. (2013) 'The role of the school nurse in child protection', *Community Practitioner*, Vol. 86, No. 12, pp. 26–9

Hall, C. (2007) 'Health visitors' and school nurses' perspectives on child protection supervision', *Community Practitioner*, Vol. 80, No. 10, pp. 26–31

Hanlon, G., Strangleman, T., Goode, J., Juff, D., O'Cathain, A. and Greatbatch, D. (2005) 'Knowledge, technology and nursing: The case of NHS Direct', *Human Relations*, Vol. 58, No. 2, pp. 147–71

Harris, J., Elcock, C., Sidebotham, P., Welbury, R. (2009) 'Safeguarding children in dentistry: 2. Do paediatric dentists neglect child dental neglect?', *British Dental Journal*, Vol. 206, No. 9, pp. 465–70

Hawkes, N. (2012) 'Proposed system to detect child abuse could deter parents from seeking treatment, pressure group says', *British Medical Journal (Clinical Research Edition)*, Vol. 345, No. 8705, pp. 1756–833

HM Government (2009) *Safeguarding Children and Young People from Sexual Exploitation*, London: Department for Children, Schools and Families

HM Government (2015) *Working Together to Safeguard Children* (online). Available from URL: www.gov.uk/government/publications/working-together-to-safeguard-children--2 (accessed 3 June 2015)

Hogg, S., Coster, D. and Brookes, H. (2015) *Baby Steps: Evidence From a Relationships-Based Perinatal Education Programme. Summary Document*, London: NSPCC

Home Office (2012) *Cross-Government Definition of Domestic Violence – A Consultation: Summary of Responses*, London: Home Office

Humphreys, C., Houghton, C. and Ellis, J. (2008) *Literature Review: Better Outcomes for Children and Young People Experiencing Domestic Abuse*, Edinburgh: Scottish Government

HVA (1994) *Protecting the Child: An HVA Guide to Practice and Procedures*, London: Health Visitors Association

Hyde, C. (2014) *Child H (Case C13) Serious Case Review: Overview Report*, Bury: Bury Safeguarding Children Board

Jay, A. (2014) *Independent Inquiry into Child Sexual Exploitation in Rotherham 1997–2013*, Rotherham: Rotherham Metropolitan Borough Council. Available from URL: www.rotherham.gov.uk/downloads/file/1407/independent_inquiry_cse_in_rotherham (accessed 18 February 2015)

Jewkes, R. (2013) 'Intimate partner violence: The end of routine screening', *The Lancet*, Vol. 382, No. 9888, pp.190–1

Jütte, S., Bentley, H., Miller, P. and Jetha, N. (2014) *How Safe Are Our Children?* London: NSPCC

Kay, J. (1999) *Protecting Children. A Practical Guide*, London: Cassell

Keeling, J. and Birch, L. (2004) 'Asking pregnant women about domestic abuse', *British Journal of Midwifery*, Vol. 12, No. 12, pp. 746–9

Kelly, A. and Symonds, A. (2003) *The Social Construction of Community Nursing*, London: Palgrave Macmillan

Kelly, N., Greaves, C., Buckland, L. and Rose, J. (2005) 'School nurses: Well placed to address challenging behaviour', *Community Practitioner*, Vol. 78, No. 3, pp. 88–92

Kemp, A. and Coles, L. (2003), 'The role of health professionals in preventing non-accidental head injury', *Child Abuse Review*, Vol. 12, No. 6, pp. 374–83

Kent, S., Dowling, M. and Byrne, G. (2011) 'Community nurses' child protection role: Views of public health nurses in Ireland', *Community Practitioner*, Vol. 84, No. 11, pp. 33–6

Keogh, B. (2013) *Review into the Quality of Care and Treatment Provided by 14 Hospital Trusts in England: Overview Report*, London: Department of Health

Kirkpatrick, S., Barlow, J., Stewart-Brown, S. and Davis, H. (2007), 'Working in partnership: User perceptions of intensive home visiting', *Child Abuse Review*, Vol. 16, No. 1, pp. 32–46; doi:10.1002/car.972

Kirtley, P. (2013) 'If you shine a light you will probably find it', report of a grass roots survey of health professionals with regard to their experiences in dealing with child sexual exploitation (online), NWG Network Tackling Child Sexual Exploitation. Available from URL: www.nhs.uk/aboutNHSChoices/professionals/healthandcareprofessionals/child-sexual-exploitation/Documents/Shine%20a%20Light.pdf (accessed 15 June 1015)

Kotter, J. (1995) 'Leading change: Why transformation efforts fail', *Harvard Business Review*, Vol. 73, No. 2, pp. 59–67

Lam, A. (2000) 'Tacit knowledge, organisational learning and societal institutions: An integrated framework', *Organisational Studies*, Vol. 21, No. 3, pp. 487–518

Laming, Lord (2009) *The Protection of Children in England: A Progress Report*, London: The Stationery Office

Lampard, K. and Marsden, E. (2015) *Themes and Lessons Learnt from NHS Investigations into Matters Relating to Jimmy Savile: Independent Report for the Secretary of State for Health*, London: Department of Health

Lane, D. and Day, P. (2001) 'Setting up a sexual health clinic in a school', *Nursing Times*, 11 October, pp. 38–9

Lawrence, A. (2004) *Principles of Child Protection. Management and Practice*, Maidenhead: Open University Press

Lazenbatt, A. Taylor, J. and Cree, L. (2009) 'A healthy settings framework: An evaluation and comparison of midwives' responses to addressing domestic violence in pregnancy', *Midwifery*, Vol. 25, pp. 622–36

Lazenbatt, A., Bunting, L. and Taylor, J. S. (2012) 'The consequences of infant maltreatment on children's future health and well-being', *British Journal of Mental Health Nursing*, Vol. 1, No. 3, pp. 171–5

Leadsom, A., Field, F., Burstow, P. and Lucas, C. (2013) 'The 1001 critical days. The importance of the conception to age two period' (online). Available from URL: www.andrealeadsom.com/downloads/1001cdmanifesto. pdf (accessed 3 January 2015)

LeBlanc, V., Regehr, C., Shlonsky, A. and Bogo, M. (2012) 'Stress responses and decision making in child protection workers faced with high conflict situations', *Child Abuse & Neglect*, Vol. 36, No. 5, pp. 404–12

Leon, D. and Walt, G. (eds) (2000) *Poverty, Inequality and Health: An International Perspective*, Oxford: Oxford University Press

Lepistö, S., Luukkaala, T. and Paavilainen, E. (2011) 'Witnessing and experiencing domestic violence: A descriptive study of adolescents', *Scandinavian Journal of Caring Sciences*, Vol. 25, No. 1, pp. 70–80

Ling, M. S. and Luker, K. (2000) 'Protecting children: Intuition and awareness in the work of health visitors', *Journal of Advanced Nursing*, Vol. 32, No. 3, pp. 572–79

Linsley, P., Kane, R. and Owen, S. (2011) *Nursing for Public Health: Promotion, Principles and Practice*, Oxford: Oxford University Press

Lister, P. G. and Crisp, B. G. (2005) 'Clinical supervision in child protection for community nurses', *Child Abuse Review*, Vol. 14, No. 1, pp. 57–72

Littler, N. (2014) 'School nurses' role in tackling child sexual exploitation', *British Journal of School Nursing*, Vol. 9, No. 10, pp. 514–5

Locke, E. A. and Latham, G. P. (2013) *New Developments in Goal Setting and Task Performance*, New York, NY: Routledge

Lombard, N. and McMillan, L. (eds) (2013) *Violence Against Women: Current Theory and Practice in Domestic Abuse, Sexual Violence and Exploitation*, London: Jessica Kingsley

Lupton, D. (1995) *The Imperative of Health: Public Health and the Regulated Body*, London: Sage

Lupton, D. A. (2011). ' "The best thing for the baby": Mothers' concepts and experiences related to promoting their infants' health and development', *Health, Risk & Society*, Vol. 13, Nos 7–8, pp. 637–51

MacMillan, H. L., Wathen, C. N., Barlow, J., Fergusson, D. M., Leventhal, J. M. and Taussig, H. N. (2009) 'Interventions to prevent child maltreatment and associated impairment', *The Lancet*, Vol. 373, No. 9658, pp. 250–66

Macvarish, J., Lee, E. and Lowe, P. (2014) 'The "first three years" movement and the infant brain: A review of critiques', *Sociology Compass*, Vol. 8, No. 6, pp. 792–804

Manning, V. (2011) *Estimates of the Numbers of Infants (Under the Age of One Year) Living with Substance Misusing Parents*. London: NSPCC

Manzano-García, G. and Ayala-Calvo, J.-C. (2014) 'An overview of nursing in Europe: A SWOT analysis', *Nursing Inquiry*, Vol. 21, No. 4, pp. 358–67;

doi:10.1111/nin.12069

Marcellus, L. (2005) 'The ethics of relation: Public health nurses and child protection clients', *Journal of Advanced Nursing*, Vol. 51, No. 4, pp. 414–20

Marmot, M., Allen, J., Goldblatt, P., Boyce, T., McNeish, D., Grady, M. and Geddes, O. (2010) *Fair Society, Healthy Lives: The Marmot Review – Strategic Review of Health Inequalities in England Post-2010*, London: UCL. Available from URL: www.marmotreview.org (accessed 15 June 2015)

Meadows, P., Tunstill, J., George, A., Dhudwar, A. and Kurtz, Z. (2011) *The Costs and Consequences of Child Maltreatment: Literature Review for the NSPCC*, London: NSPCC. Available from URL: www.nspcc.org.uk/globalassets/documents/research-reports/costs-and-consequences-child-maltreatment.pdf (accessed 15 June 2015)

Melrose, M. (2013) 'Twenty-first century party people: Young people and sexual exploitation in the new millennium', *Child Abuse Review*, Vol. 22, No. 3, pp. 155–68

Mezey, G., Bacchus, L., Haworth, A. and Bewley, S. (2003) 'Midwives' perceptions and experiences of routine enquiry for domestic violence', *BJOG: An International Journal of Obstetrics and Gynaecology*, Vol. 110, No. 8, pp. 744–52

Min, M. O., Minnes, S., Kim, H. and Singer, L. T. (2013) 'Pathways linking childhood maltreatment and adult physical health', *Child Abuse & Neglect*, Vol. 37, No. 6, pp. 361–73

Ministry of Justice (2014) 'Deaths among children' (online). Available from URL: www.turvallisuustutkinta.fi/material/attachments/otkes/tutkintaselostukset/fi/muutonnettomuudet/2012/AtKr3zBTr/Y2012-S1_Lasten_kuolemat.pdf (accessed 21 May 2014)

Ministry of Social Affairs and Health (2013) 'Child and family policy in Finland: Brochures' (online). Available from URL: www.julkari.fi/handle/10024/104419 (accessed 13 July 2015)

Mitcheson, J. and Cowley, S. (2003) 'Empowerment or control? An analysis of the extent to which client participation is enabled during health visitor/client interactions using a structured health needs assessment tool', *International Journal of Nursing Studies*, Vol. 40, pp. 413–26

Montalvo-Liendo, N. (2009) 'Cross-cultural factors in disclosure of intimate partner violence: An integrated review', *Journal of Advanced Nursing*, Vol. 65, No. 1, pp. 20–34

Montalvo-Liendo, N., Wardell, D. W., Engebretson, J. and Reininger, B. M. (2009) 'Factors influencing disclosure of abuse by women of Mexican descent', *Journal of Nursing Scholarship*, Vol. 41, No. 4, pp. 359–67

Moullin, S., Waldfogel, J. and Washbrook, E. (2014) *Baby Bonds. Parenting, Attachment and a Secure Base for Children*, London: The Sutton Trust

Mummery, S. (2002) 'Influences on registered nurses' decision-making in cases of suspected child abuse – Relevance and implications for UK practice', *Child Abuse Review*, Vol. 11, No. 3, pp. 179–81

Munro, E. (2007) *Child Protection*, London: Sage Munro, E. (2011a) *The Munro Review of Child Protection. Interim Report: The Child's Journey*, London: Department for Education

Munro, E. (2011) *The Munro Review of Child Protection. Final Report: A Child-Centred System*, cmd 8062, London: Department for Education

Munro, E. R. and Manful, E. (2012*)* 'Safeguarding children: A comparison of England's data with that of Australia, Norway and the United States', Research brief DFE-RB198 (online). Available from URL: www.gov.uk/government/publications/safeguarding-children-a-comparison-of-englands-data-with-that-of-australia-norway-and-the-united-states (accessed 5 January 2015)

Murphy, E. (2003) 'Expertise and forms of knowledge in the government of families', *The Sociological Review*, Vol. 51, No. 4, pp. 433–62

Murray, L. (2014) *The Psychology of Babies. How Relationships Support Development From Birth To Two*, London: Constable & Robinson

Naish, J. and Cloke, C. (1992) *Key Issues in Child Protection for Health Visitors and Nurses*, Harlow: Longman.

National Advisory Group on the Safety of Patients in England (2013) *A Promise to Learn – A Commitment to Act: Improving the Safety of Patients in England*, London: Williams Lea

National Collaborating Centre for Women's and Children's Health (2009) *When to Suspect Child Maltreatment* (commissioned by NICE), London: RCOG Press. Available from URL: www.nice.org.uk/nicemedia/pdf/CG89FullGuideline.pdf (accessed 3 January 2015)

NCB (2013) *Greater Expectations: Raising Aspirations for Our Children*, London: National Children's Bureau. Available from URL: http://ncb.org.uk/media/1032641/greater-expectations.pdf (accessed 6 March 2015)

Nelson, C. A., Furtado, E. A., Fox, N. A. and Zeanah, C. H. (2009) 'The deprived human brain', *American Scientist*, Vol. 97, pp. 222–9

Nettleton, S. and Bunton, R. (1995) 'Sociological critiques of health promotion', in Bunton, R., Burrows, R. and Nettleton, S. (eds) (1995) *The Sociology of Health Promotion*, London: Routledge, pp. 41–58

NHS Commissioning Board (2013) *Safeguarding Vulnerable People in the Reformed NHS. Accountability and Assurance Framework*, London: NHS Commissioning Board. Available from URL: www.england.nhs.uk/wp-content/uploads/2013/03/safeguarding-vulnerable-people.pdf (accessed 13 ~July 2015)

NHS England (2014) *2015–16 National Heath Visiting Core Service Specification*, London: NHS England

NHS Institute for Innovation and Improvement (2008) 'Quality and service improvement tools: SBAR' (online). Available from URL: www.institute.nhs.uk/quality_and_service_improvement_tools/quality_and_service_improvement_tools/sbar_-_situation_-_background_-_assessment_-_recommendation.html (accessed 13 February 2015)

NICE (2014a) *Health Visiting: NICE Local Government Briefings*, London: National Institute for Health and Clinical Excellence

NICE (2014b) 'Domestic violence and abuse: How health services, social care and the organisations they work with can respond effectively' (online). Available from URL: http://publications.nice.org.uk/

domestic-violence-and-abuse-how-health-services-social-care-and-the-organisations-they-work-with-ph50 (accessed 3 January 2015)

NMC (2008) *The Code: Standards of Conduct, Performance and Ethics for Nurses and Midwives,* London: Nursing and Midwifery Council

NMC (2010) *Standards for Competence for Registered Nurses,* London: Nursing and Midwifery Council

NMC (2015) 'The code. Professional standards of practice and behaviour for nurses and midwives' (online). Available from URL: www.nmc-uk.org/Documents/NMC-Publications/NMC-Code-A5-FINAL.pdf (accessed 13 February 2015)

Norman, R. E., Byambaa, M., De, R., Butchart, A., Scott, J. and Vos, T. (2012) 'The long-term health consequences of child physical abuse, emotional abuse, and neglect', *PLOS Medicine,* Vol. 9, No. 11, pp. e1001349; doi:10.1371/journal.pmed.1001349

O'Donnell, M., Scott, D. and Stanley, F. (2008) 'Child abuse and neglect – is it time for a public health approach?', *Australian and New Zealand Journal of Public Health,* Vol. 32, No. 4, pp. 325–30

Ofsted (2011) *Good Practice by Local Safeguarding Children Boards,* London: Office for Standards in Education, Children's Services and Skills

Owen, G. (1977) *Health Visiting,* London: Baillière Tindall

Oxfordshire Safeguarding Children Board (2015) 'Serious case review into child sexual exploitation in Oxfordshire: From the experiences of Children A, B, C, D, E, and F' (online). Available from URL: www.oscb.org.uk/wp-content/uploads/SCR-into-CSE-in-Oxfordshire-FINAL-FOR-WEBSITE.pdf (accessed 6 March 2015)

Paavilainen, E. and Flinck, A. (2013) 'National clinical nursing guideline for identifying and intervening in child maltreatment within the family in Finland', *Child Abuse Review,* Vol. 22, No. 3, pp. 209–20

Paavilainen, E. and Flinck, A. (2014) 'The effectiveness of methods designed to identify child maltreatment in social and health care: A systematic review protocol', *JBI Library of Systematic Reviews and Implementation Reports,* Vol. 12, pp. 90–100

Parker, S. and Kirk, S. A. (2006) 'The parent positive programme: Opportunities for health visiting', *Community Practitioner,* Vol. 79, No. 1, pp. 10–14

Parsons, C., Young, K., Murray, L., Stein, A. and Kringelbach, M. (2010) 'The functional neuroanatomy of the evolving parent-infant relationship', *Progress in Neurobiology,* Vol. 91, No. 3, pp. 220–41

Parton, N. (1991) *Governing the Family. Child Care, Child Protection and the State,* Basingstoke: Macmillan

Parton, N. (2006) *Safeguarding Childhood: Early Intervention and Surveillance in a Late Modern Society,* Basingstoke: Palgrave Macmillan

Parton, N. (2014) *The Politics of Child Protection: Contemporary Developments and Future Directions,* London: Palgrave Macmillan

Parton, N., Thorpe, D. and Wattam, C. (1997) *Child Protection: Risk and the Moral Order,* Basingstoke: Macmillan

Peckover, S. (2002) 'Supporting and policing mothers: An analysis of the disciplinary practices of health visiting', *Journal of Advanced Nursing,* Vol. 38,

No. 4, pp. 369–77

Peckover, S. (2003) ' "I could have just done with a little more help": An analysis of women's help-seeking from health visitors in the context of domestic violence', *Health and Social Care in the Community,* Vol. 11, No. 3, pp. 275–82

Peckover, S. (2009) 'Health and safeguarding children: An "Expansionary project" or "good practice"?', in *Critical Perspectives on Safeguarding Children,* Chichester: Wiley, pp. 149–70

Peckover, S. (2013) 'From "public health" to "safeguarding children": British health visiting in policy, practice and research', *Children and Society,* Vol. 27, No. 2, pp. 116–26

Peckover, S. and Smith, S. (eds) (2011) 'Public health approaches to safeguarding children', *Child Abuse Review,* Vol. 20, No. 4, pp. 231–7

Peckover, S. and Trotter, F. (2014), 'Keeping the focus on children: The challenges of safeguarding children affected by domestic abuse', *Health & Social Care in the Community,* Vol. 23, No. 4, pp. 399–407; doi:10.1111/hsc.12160

Peckover, S., Smith, S. and Wondergem, F. (2013) 'Doing "serious case reviews": The views and experiences of NHS named and designated safeguarding children professionals', *Child Abuse Review*; doi:10.1002/car.2301

Petersen, A. and Lupton, D. (1996) *The New Public Health,* London: Sage

PHE (2014) *From Evidence Into Action: Opportunities to Protect and Improve the Nation's Health,* London: Public Health England

PHE (2015) *Rapid Review to Update Evidence for the Healthy Child Programme 0–5,* London: Public Health England

Powell, C. (2007) *Safeguarding Children and Young People: A Guide for Nurses and Midwives,* Maidenhead: Open University Press

Powell, C. (2011) *Safeguarding and Child Protection for Nurses, Midwives and Health Visitors: A Practical Guide,* Maidenhead, Open University Press

Powell, C. and Appleton, J, (2012) 'Children and young people's missed health care appointments: Reconceptualising "not attend" to "was not brought" – A review of the evidence for practice', *Journal of Research in Nursing,* Vol. 17, No. 2, pp. 181–92

Radford, L., Corral, S., Bradley, C., Fisher, H., Bassett, C., Howat, N. and Collishaw, S. (2011) *Child Abuse & Neglect in the UK Today,* London: NSPCC

Radford, L., Corral, S., Bradley, C. and Fisher, H. L. (2013) 'The prevalence and impact of child maltreatment and other types of victimization in the UK: Findings from a population survey of caregivers, children and young people and young adults', *Child Abuse & Neglect,* Vol. 37, No. 10, pp. 801–13

Ramsay, J., Carter, Y., Davidson, L., Dunne, D., Eldridge, S., Hegarty, K., Rivas, C., Taft, A., Warburton, A. and Feder, G. (2009) 'Advocacy interventions to reduce or eliminate violence and promote the physical and psychosocial well-being of women who experience intimate partner abuse', *Cochrane Database of Systematic Reviews*; doi:10.1002/14651858.CD005043.pub2

Ranson, K. E. and Urichuk, L. J. (2008) 'The effect of parent-child attachment relationships on child biopsychosocial outcomes: A review', *Early Child*

Development and Care, Vol. 178, No. 2, pp. 129–52

RCN (2003) *Defining Nursing,* London: Royal College of Nursing

RCN (2012) *The RCN's UK Position on School Nursing,* London: Royal College of Nursing

RCPCH (2014) *Safeguarding Children and Young People: Roles and Competences for Healthcare Staff,* intercollegiate guidance 3rd edn, London: Royal College of Paediatrics and Child Health

Reder, P. and Duncan, S. (2003) 'Understanding communication in child protection networks', *Child Abuse Review,* Vol. 12, No. 2, pp. 82–100

Reed, H. (2012) *In the Eye of the Storm: Britain's Forgotten Children and Families,* a research report for Action for Children, The Children's Society and NSPCC, London: Landman Economics

Roper, N., Logan, W. and Tiernay, A. (1996) *The Elements of Nursing: A Model for Nursing Based on a Model for Living,* Edinburgh: Churchill Livingstone

Rouse, S. (2002) 'Protecting children: The role of the health visitor', in Wilson, K. and James, A. (eds) (2002) *The Child Protection Handbook,* Edinburgh: Baillière Tindall

Ruston, A. M. (2006), 'Interpreting and managing risk in a machine bureaucracy: Professional decision-making in NHS Direct', *Health, Risk and Society,* Vol. 8, No. 3, pp. 257–71

Saied-Tessier, A. (2014) *Estimating the Costs of Child Sexual Abuse in the UK,* London: NSPCC

Schore, A. (2001) 'The effects of early relational trauma on right brain development, affect regulation, and infant mental health', *Infant Mental Health Journal,* Vol. 22, Nos 1–2, pp. 201–69

Scottish Government (2011) *A New Look at Hall 4: The Early Years Good Health for Every Child,* Edinburgh: Scottish Government. Available from URL: www.gov.scot/resource/doc/337318/0110676.pdf (accessed 3 June 2015)

Scottish Government (2012) *A Guide To Getting It Right For Every Child,* Edinburgh: Scottish Government. Available from URL: www.scotland.gov.uk/Resource/0045/00458341.pdf (accessed 3 June 2015)

Scottish Government (2014a) '500 new health visitors' (online). Available from URL: http://news.scotland.gov.uk/News/500-new-health-visitors-ddc.aspx (accessed 3 June 2015)

Scottish Government (2014b) *Children and Young People (Scotland) Bill,* Edinburgh: Scottish Government

Scullin, K. and Galloway, S. (2014) 'Challenges from the frontline. Supporting families with multiple adversities in a time of austerity', a report in collaboration with Barnardos/NSPCC Scotland. Available from URL: www.nspcc.org.uk/Inform/research/findings/multiple-adversities-report_wdf103854.pdf (accessed 15 June 2015)

Segal, L. and Dalziel, K. (2011) 'Investing to protect our children: Using economics to derive an evidence-based strategy', *Child Abuse Review,* Vol. 20, No. 4, pp. 274–89

Sidebotham, P. (2012) 'What do serious case reviews achieve?', *Archives of Disease in Childhood,* Vol. 97, No. 3, pp. 189–92

Sidebotham, P. (2013) 'Authoritative child protection', *Child Abuse Review*, Vol. 22, No. 1, pp. 1–4

Smith, S. (2010) 'Helping parents cope with crying babies: Decision-making and interaction at NHS Direct', *Journal of Advanced Nursing*, Vol. 66, No. 2, pp. 381–91

Spangaro, J., Poulos, R. and Zwi, A. (2011) 'Pandora doesn't live here anymore: Normalization of screening for intimate partner violence in Australian antenatal, mental health and substance abuse services', *Violence and Victims*, Vol. 26, pp. 130–44

Spinney, A. (2013) 'Safe from the start? An action research project on early intervention materials for children affected by domestic and family violence', *Children and Society*, Vol. 27, No. 5, pp. 397–405

Stokes, J. and Schmidt, G. (2012) 'Child protection decision-making: A factorial analysis using case vignettes', *Social Work*, Vol. 57, pp. 83–90

Taket, A., Nurse, J., Smith, K., Watson, J., Shakespeare, J., Lavis, V., Cosgrove, K., Mulley, K. and Feder, G. (2003) 'Routinely asking women about domestic violence in health settings', *British Medical Journal*, Vol. 327, pp. 673–76

Taylor, C. and White, S. (2000) *Practising Reflexivity in Health and Welfare: Making Knowledge*, Buckingham: Open University Press

Taylor, J. S., Lauder, W., Corlett, J. and Moy, M. (2009) 'Practitioner assessments of "good enough" parenting: Factorial survey', *Journal of Clinical Nursing*, Vol. 18, pp. 1180–9

Taylor, J., Bradbury-Jones, C., Kroll, T. and Duncan, F. (2013) 'Health professionals' beliefs about domestic abuse and the issue of disclosure: A critical incident technique study', *Health & Social Care in the Community*, Vol. 2, No. 5, pp. 489–99

Taylor-Gooby, P. (2012). 'Root and branch restructuring to achieve major cuts: The social policy programme of the 2010 UK Coalition Government', *Social Policy & Administration*. Vol. 46, No. 1, pp. 61–82

Tickell, C. (2011) *The Early Years: Foundations for Life, Health and Learning – An Independent Report on the Early Years Foundation Stage to Her Majesty's Government*, London: Department for Education

Tod, A. and Hirst, J. (2014) *Health and Inequality: Applying Public Health Research to Policy and Practice*, London: Routledge

Underdown, A. and Barlow, J. (2012) 'Promoting infant mental health: A public health priority and approach', in Miller, L. and Hevey, D. (eds) (2012), *Policy Issues in the Early Years*, London: Sage

Valencia-Rojas, N., Lawrence, H. P. and Goodman, D. (2008) 'Prevalence of early childhood caries in a population of children with history of maltreatment', *Journal of Public Health Dentistry*, Vol. 68, No. 2, pp. 94–101

Vincent, C. (2010) *Patient Safety*, Chichester: Wiley-Blackwell

Wastell, D. and White, S. (2012) 'Blinded by neuroscience: Social policy, the family and the infant brain', *Families, Relationships and Society*, Vol. 1, No. 3, pp. 397–414

Watkins, D. and Cousins, J. (eds) (2010) *Public Health and Community Nursing: Frameworks for Practice*, Edinburgh: Churchill Livingstone

Watson, G. and Rodwell, S. (eds) (2014) *Safeguarding and Protecting Children,*

Young People and Families. A Guide for Nurses and Midwives, London: Sage

WAVE Trust (2013) *Conception to Age 2: The Age of Opportunity,* Croydon: WAVE Trust

Weick, K. (1995) 'Organizational redesign as improvisation', in Huber, G. and Glick, W. (eds) (1995) *Organizational Change and Redesign,* New York, NY: Oxford University Press, pp. 346–79

Welsh Assembly (2004) 'Children and young people: Rights to action' (online). Available from http://gov.wales/docs/caecd/publications/090415r ightstoactionen.pdf

West, M., Eckert, R., Steward K. and Pasmore, B. (2014) *Developing Collective Leadership for Health Care,* London: Kings Fund

White, S. and Stancombe, J. (2003), *Clinical Judgement in the Health and Welfare Professions: Extending the Evidence Base,* Buckingham: Open University Press

White, S., Wastell, D., Smith, S., Hall, C., Whitaker, E., Debelle, G., Mannion, R. and Waring, J. (2015) 'Improving practice in safeguarding at the interface between hospital services and children's social care: A mixed-methods case study', *Health Service Delivery Research,* Vol. 3, No. 4; doi:10.3310/hsdr03040. Available from URL: www.journalslibrary.nihr.ac.uk/hsdr/volume-3/issue-4#abstract (accessed 9 March 2015)

Whittaker, K. A. and Cowley, S. (2012) 'A survey of parental self-efficacy experiences: Maximising potential through health visiting and universal parenting support', *Journal of Clinical Nursing,* Vol. 21, No. 21–2, pp. 3276–86

WHO (2006) *Preventing Child Maltreatment: A Guide to Taking Action and Generating Evidence,* Geneva: World Health Organization and International Society for Prevention of Child Abuse & Neglect

WHO (2007) *Preventing Child Maltreatment in Europe: A Public Health Approach. Policy Briefing,* a violence and injury prevention programme, Denmark: World Health Organization regional office for Europe

WHO (2013) *European Report on Preventing Child Maltreatment,* Copenhagen: World Health Organization

WHO, United Nations Office on Drugs and Crime and United Nations Development Programme (2014) *Global Status Report on Violence Prevention 2014.* Geneva: World Health Organization

Wilson, C., Thompson, L., McConnachie, A. and Wilson, P. (2011) 'Matching parenting support needs to service provision in a universal 13-month child health surveillance visit', *Child: Care, Health and Development,* Vol. 38, No. 5, pp. 665–74; doi:10.111/j.1365–2214.2011.01315.x

Wolfe, I., Macfarlane, A., Donkin, A., Marmot, M. and Viner, R. (2014) *Why Children Die: Death in Infants, Children, and Young People in the UK – Part A,* London: Royal College of Paediatrics and Child Health and National Children's Bureau

Women's Aid (2015) *Women's Aid Annual Survey 2014: Domestic Violence Services in England,* Bristol: Women's Aid

Woodman, J. and Gilbert, R. (2013) 'Proposed child protection information system seems to run counter to best evidence' [Letter to the editor], *British*

Medical Journal; doi:10.1136/bmj.f504

Woodman, J., Pitt, M. and Wentz, R. (2008) 'Performance of screening tests for child physical abuse in accident and emergency departments', *Health Technology Assessment*, Vol. 12, No. 33, pp.1–95

Woodman, J., Lecky, F. and Hodes, D. (2010) 'Screening injured children for physical abuse of neglect in emergency departments: A systematic review', *Child Care Health and Development*, Vol. 36, No. 2, pp. 153–64

Woodman, J., Hodson, D., Gardner, R., Cuthbert, C., Woolley, A., Allister, J., Rafi, I., de Lusignan, S. and Gilbert, R. (2014) *The GP's Role in Responding to Child Maltreatment*, London: NSPCC

Wright, C. M., Jeffrey, S. K., Ross, M. K., Wallis, L. and Wood, R. (2009) 'Targeting health visitor care: Lessons from "Starting well"', *Archives of Disease in Childhood*, Vol. 94, pp. 23–7

Wyness, M. (2012) *Childhood and Society* (2nd edn) Basingstoke: Palgrave Macmillan

Zolotor, A. and Puzia, M. (2010) 'Bans against corporal punishment: A systematic review of the laws, changes in attitudes and behaviours', *Child Abuse Review*, Vol. 19, No. 4, pp. 229–47

INDEX

Note: page numbers in *italics* refer to figures or tables